The Lesbian Housewyfe: Bigger, Broader, Delightfuller

LuckyChix Press

LA Bourgeois

Cover Graphic Design by Stephanie Reineke

Lesbian Housewyfe Character Art by Carolina Gryffin

Find Carolina Gryffin on Instagram at @gryffinpoodles.

Versions of the following essays were originally published on OutFrontMagazine.com: Rainbow Hair Fix, Are You Watching the Pageantry, Alert for Democracy, Who's the Chainsaw-Wielding Demon Now, Psychic Jeopardy, Paranoid or Reasonable

CONTENTS

·♥·♥·♥·♥·♥·

Things You Need To Know

My wife and I moved from Steamboat Springs, Colorado to Asheville, North Carolina at the end of 2016.

In 2017, my wife had a stroke. In the aftermath, taking a job as an office manager and bookkeeper kept us secure and felt like a cozy choice for me. But by 2019, the inevitable discontent in working for someone else emerged. When the pandemic closed most offices in North Carolina, I began working from home and never returned to that job-job.

The Lesbian Housewyfe reintroduced herself in 2021. "Why not start writing about me again?" she asked while sipping a cocktail and knitting. "What have you got to lose? Let's have some fun!"

·♥·♥·♥·♥·♥·

GENDER IS A SPECTRUM

I went to a business mixer a week after the immunity kicked in from my first completed COVID vaccine. It was the first evening I'd been out networking in at least two years. I was nervous; I didn't know what to expect. There were so many people on the lawn of this gorgeous event venue. I pretended we were all attending a garden party and resolved to make friends.

As I talked to a couple of fellows, I thought, "Oh! My people! It's so nice to have a regular conversation with another gay person."

And then they would mention their wives (once she was standing right next to him!).

I felt good about my response as I managed to keep the surprise off my face (except maybe I got surprised eyes? I could have had surprised eyes), thinking, "Gender is a spectrum. Gender is a spectrum."

You see, I've met so many gay straight people.

So. Many.

I came out in the fall of 1992 and, along with electing Bill Clinton, the state where I lived passed an amendment to their constitution that allowed active discrimination against gay people. While I navigated the waters of my new queer community, I watched my friends hide their sexuality from their families and co-workers. Immersed in the theater, my circle contained more out gay people than others, but the norm was still to hide ourselves.

Because of this, I learned quickly about "gaydar," the mysterious force that points you toward other lesbian and gay people. Those little tells that reveal the possibility of a connection. While people might be out to their inner circle of friends, they rarely outed themselves to their family and workplace. Even today, that path contains the possibility of destroying familial connections and livelihoods.

As such, while observing people at parties and on talk shows, we would guess who was gay and hiding it. Soooooooooo much fun! Celebrities, of course, were the major topic, but as the wine flowed, so did our mouths, and we would make assertions about friends and family too. These were the people who set off our gaydar but maintained actively straight lifestyles.

"When do you think he'll come out and get divorced from her?"

"Well, you just know they're both gay. I wonder if they even ever had sex."

"She joined our softball team and keeps giving Joyce these longing looks but insists she's not gay. Whyyyyyyy? They could be so happy together!"

Watching for the tells and then asserting our correctness when the person finally came out was exhilarating! And when it was a celebrity? Oh! The "See, I told you so's" dropped from our lips like a refreshing rain!

Plus, each new person asserting their homosexuality felt like another addition to our team. Another voice joining our ongoing battle for civil rights and the recognition of our humanity.

In those days, the chance that someone who had that little extra something in their manner was gay was pretty high, because you would only take that risk if you wanted to communicate your availability. Revealing yourself to find that connection was dangerous, as we saw with the martyrdom of Matthew Shepard (along with many, many others).

Back then, when I talked of meeting gay straight people, I was talking about meeting gay people who lived straight lives.

Now, of course, the sea has changed. A massive tide pulled us through that long, wretched time. As always, tide pools and quicksand remain to snag us, but those moments feel fewer and farther between. The young folks today don't put up with the bullshit we took for granted. They force the conversation around free-flowing gender and sexualities, taking the legacy of the fight we started and punching it forward.

And now, when I talk about gay straight people, I mean straight people who do and say things that make my gaydar ping with such intensity that I expect them to start farting rainbows.

One dear, dear friend of mine is the gayest straight man I'll ever know, and his devotion to his wife has carried them through many hard times. I think it has to do with the fact that he's so comfortable in himself, willing to express both his masculine and feminine sides.

His wife's brother and his husband agree with me. Leaning in at a graduation party, they confided, "Gayest straight man I've ever met. And we live in San Francisco."

Case closed.

Another friend tries hard to get the job of "gayest straight man I know" with his propensity to pull out drag at the drop of a hat. However, he's an actor, and his closet contains oodles of costumes including Batman and Indiana Jones, alongside Marilyn Monroe. I would say he's more addicted to dressing up than drawn to drag. Plus, his eyes light up with sparkly stars each time his drop-dead gorgeous wife comes into view. No hiding that look.

For those few years I worked for my local arts council, I ran the box office for one of their main fundraisers, a Follies-style show of funny skits and songs. During the performance, actors hung out in the lobby area with me as they waited to go onstage. One night, this fellow strode out of the green room completely done. The dress, the makeup, the wig, the heels—all fit the occasion. He flounced over to my little table and began chatting. "Oh my," I said. "Look at you."

He preened. He really is a gorgeous lady.

"You could be the gayest straight man I know."

His smile faltered just a little.

"But someone else has got you beat."

Delighted, he zipped off for his next entrance.

With my move to North Carolina, however, I'm meeting so many gay straight folks just wandering out in the wild that I find myself in conversation with someone thinking, "You're married to a woman?!" and "Sure. What's your husband's name? Charlotte?"

Oh, my brain is so snarky!

But today on the lawn at the networking event, I held steady. "Gender is a spectrum. Gender is a spectrum."

A young friend of mine, a person I crocheted an afghan for when they were born, amazed me when they came out as non-binary. The sheer audacity of rejecting gender took my breath away. I couldn't imagine such a thing, growing up in the Arkansas heat. Simply embracing my pansexuality took a leap, and discovering that I had deeper connections with women than with men somehow seemed like a breach of etiquette. After using the proper fork my whole life, I'd found that I preferred to use the salad fork to eat my steak.

But to throw away the place setting entirely? I marveled at this young person. When they visited, they thanked us for using their preferred pronouns, sharing tales of relatives who didn't even try. That casual cruelty seemed a slap in the face to me, but this graceful individual took it in stride and I followed their lead.

And so, I've been working on my thoughts and words. Asking people and noting their preferred pronouns. Knowing that using those pronouns expresses kindness, respect, and love.

These days, when my gaydar starts pinging, I wind it back. Not that everyone is out of the closet, but with less reason than ever to stay there and views of who we can be in the world expanding all the time, my preferred way of being is to allow the person their own view of their sexuality and gender.

Gender is a spectrum.

Even if your wife's name should be Larry.

·♥·♥·♥·♥·♥·

THE RETIREMENT OF THE GREAT HUNTRESS

My tortoiseshell Maine Coon mix, Dolce, used to catch the mice before they even entered the house. The Great Huntress, as she demanded to be called, left little body parts around our property like an untidy serial killer. A pile of feathers. The remains of a vole outside the front door. "We need a little mousie chalk outline," I would yell to Stephanie. She disposed of the bodies.

No mouse dared to sleep in our house.

Now she's about to turn 17, and her main activities are sleeping in sunspots, eating, and demanding pets and treats. She pops up onto the couch beside me as I knit and snags my hand with one long claw, pulling it toward her head. "Oh, you want lovings," I cry, delighted even as she scratches a red line across my knuckle. I plunge my hand into her soft belly fur and ruffle and rub and give her the pets she desires. Then I return to my knitting, rejoicing that she chose me to snuggle and injure.

The Great Huntress has retired.

I suspected mice were back when I heard strange clunkings and clankings in the kitchen late at night.

You see, there's been so much rain. So. Much. Rain. And during the rain, mice enter my home. They zip in through little holes and the main door when we leave it open for the pets.

The whole family was curled together in the bedroom. Another thunk alerted Dolce. Ears pointed and eyes narrowing, she stalked out into the kitchen. A small crash and a scurry across the floor told me the hunt was on.

The next morning, a mouse lay dead in our master bathroom. Sprawled at the base of the toilet, it appeared to have died more from fright than anything else. (Though I didn't study it for tooth marks. What am I, kitty CSI?) Like most retirees, the Great Huntress couldn't resist a chase, but she's not up for the down-and-dirty part of the job.

Of course, one mouse means more. Sure enough, mouse poop turned up in the cracks and crevices of the counters, at the edges of baskets, and under towels. Yuck!

Time to pull out the live mouse trap.

A little peanut butter baited the trap. I settled it on the favorite mouse route that evening and turned off the light. The door slapped closed about ten minutes later.

Gotcha.

Padding out into the kitchen, I turned on the light to find Dolce standing over the green tube, reaching her paw out to knock it into the middle of the kitchen floor. As far as I can tell, slapping the trap across the smooth floor brings her more joy than catching the mice these days. It's like a labor-saving device. She looks up at me as if to say, "Did you know? It's miraculous! It catches the mice and then I can play with them for hours!"

Ah, the wonders of technology!

I left her playing for a moment while I retrieved a dishtowel. Dropping it over the top of the trap, I scooped the whole thing up and put it on the dryer in the laundry room.

Wrapping the trap with a towel protects surfaces from the mouse droppings. Plus, the darkness keeps the mouse calm.

Dolce sprawled across my space on the sheets when I returned to bed. So satisfied with herself. Looking at me as if to say, "And that's how a professional does it. Thanks for cleaning up."

I know. I'm fooling myself to think she thanked me.

When I woke up the next morning, the mouse and I took a drive while Dolce cuddled with Stephanie. We circled around until I found a sort-of deserted area just over a mile away from our house (the minimum distance required to keep the mouse from finding their way back). Saying a prayer of blessing and encouragement, I tumbled the animal out of the tube into the grass.

They gave me the little mousie finger and sprinted off.

When I live-trap these mice and relocate them, I'm sending them out into the arena for their real-life Hunger Games. However, in my area, finding a field at least a mile away from any other home is a challenge I've yet to overcome, so they have a good chance of relocating into another house. We humans packed ourselves into these hills, all of us wanting our one-to-three acre plots. My best hope is that the mice get to live their regular little lives, eaten by a fox or some other mouse-eating varmint instead of slinking into a house that uses killing traps.

Especially the sticky traps. Don't use those! What an awful way to go!

The telltale sound of mice thumping into the dog food bowl woke me in the dark. As I tried to go back to sleep, Dolce alerted us to the hunt with a series of peeping meows and the uncertain crackle of a cat trying to sneak through a series of plastic bags and broom bristles.

Losing speed and grace in her old age was what sent the Great Huntress into retirement, so I shouldn't be surprised at waking up.

However...

Trying to stay sleepy, I wrestled her out of the broom closet and dumped her back on the bed. She cuddled in, content to allow the mouse to zip back to their hiding place.

Mice show up in pairs, so I knew I had at least one more catch-and-release adventures ahead.

As I caught-and-released, repeating the process over several days as mouse after mouse appeared, a gas crisis hit. I laughed when Stephanie told me about missed gas deliveries and lines at gas stations. Surely, this wasn't so dire.

The next morning, I drove my mouse out in a new direction.

I go in new directions so they can't find each other and share information on how to return.

Along my route, a line of traffic at a gas station trailed into the highway. A group of computer hackers (What do you call a group of hackers? A nerd of hackers? A code of hackers? I should know this!) had broken into the system of the local gas supplier and somehow prevented the gas from arriving at stations. Panic spread across the region. Trucks and cars blocked the opposite lane as I passed them. Red gas cans packed the beds of pickup trucks. Later I saw a video online showing a woman filling a plastic bag with gasoline, dragging it back to her car while sloshing gas all over the ground.

Note to everyone: Don't Do That!

I reflexively checked the gauge. A little over half a tank. I work from home and rarely drive, filling my tank once a month instead of once a week. They were predicting the pipeline and subsequent delivery system would be resolved by the middle of the next week.

The mouse scuffled across the rocking floor of the trap, clicking the plastic back and forth. I pulled onto a side road and lingered at a lonely stop sign to grab the mouse and tumble them out onto the grass.

That damn cat! I thought. She could catch these mice herself instead of waiting for the trap to contain them, waking me up with the scratching slide of the plastic across the floor. I'm spending all my gas driving these mice into the country!

Now the mouse-release adventure evolved into a thriller. Would I run out of mice or gas first? I combined trips. Release the mouse on the way to the chiropractor, but not so near the chiropractor that they would show up at that house. Release the mouse in the park as I walk to the library to pick up books I have on hold.

When I dropped off the last mouse into the grass next to a highway exit, the gas tank was just under half and the waits at stations had reduced from hours to minutes.

I won this round, little mousies.

Now stay away from my house! Don't you know there's a retired assassin inside?

I hope she cuddles with me tonight!

· ♥ · ♥ · ♥ · ♥ · ♥ ·

BUBBLES TO THE RESCUE!

I do not bake beautiful bread. My loaves, before baking and after, are not "Instagram worthy." Artfully arranged slashes, interesting shapes, and vegetation don't make an appearance in my bread-baking process.

During the pandemic, social media was bursting with beautiful loaves, before-and-after pictures of yeasty art. When I needed a break from outrage about the political shitshow, scrolling #sourdough delighted me with inventive shapes and colors. Jealousy warred with admiration of the perfect displays.

Despite its aesthetic lack, my bread is tasty, nutritious, and an intrinsic part of my life. Once every two weeks, I pull a sourdough starter out of the refrigerator and bake two loaves of bread for our household. Those loaves are sturdy and practical, used for slices fresh from the oven with soft butter, French toast on the weekends, and gifting occasional chunks to my mother-in-law. We average eating a loaf a week. My wife mostly stays away from the carbs(!), so the French toast is (usually) all mine.

Indulging in French toast every weekend started during the pandemic.

Along with a flour and then yeast shortage.

When the yeast disappeared from the shelves of the grocery stores,

I felt the call of every superhero. Time to save the planet!

Or, at least, my little corner of the planet!

Or, at least, those folks who didn't have a friend with a sourdough starter.

Yep. All of those baking newbies who'd bought ALL the flour now needed yeast.

Diatribe

JUST because they got stuck at home with NOTHING BETTER TO DO, they began baking and hoarding flour. FLOUR! Making life hard for all of us who regularly bake bread! Who do it because we LOVE BAKING FIRST! NOT because we are BORED! WHY am I searching for the flour I NEED to bake the bread to feed my family LIKE USUAL just so you can PLAY Holly Homesteader with your fancy new bread machine you bought online YESTERDAY?!?!

Diatribe Over

Excuse me. That just slipped out. It happens when your filter gets flushed away by menopausal hot flashes.

Because *I* am a GOOD and KIND person who doesn't HOARD NECESSITIES, I took pity on these yeastless newbies.

I'd been looking for a way to help as the pandemic crept across the country. With little time, less money, and a wife who ticked off way too many "vulnerable population" boxes, at first I couldn't see a way.

But now. Now, I had yeast.

More specifically, I had a hundred-year-old Colorado sourdough starter.

When I first received the starter from a young friend (he knew I baked bread and wouldn't I just love to have some?), I smiled tensely and thought, "God! Another thing to keep alive." But over the years, the starter and I became friends. Her name is "Bubbles."

Don't blame me for the bad pun! She named herself.

She shares her yeast with me and stays alive despite my occasional lapses in regular feeding. Her resilience comes from the fact that she was born in the Rocky Mountains and her ability to hibernate in the freezer for months. That's how she got across the country with me from Colorado, frozen solid and transferred to our most valiant portable cooler just before pulling away from our old home. For four days, she slowly defrosted as we drove. Upon arrival, I revived her and proudly displayed a picture of the first North Carolina loaf on social media.

During the time right after my wife's stroke, Bubbles aided and abetted my anger. Slamming dough against the counter released the fury at this new twist my life had taken. Smelling the bread baking and then consuming slices of the fresh hot loaf comforted me.

In happier times, she experimented with me. We created dinner rolls and pizza crust together. Each time I pull up another sourdough recipe on the internet, her soul perches on my shoulder and gives me encouragement.

Bubbles is my baking soulmate. She's my special girl.

And she could help all of these yeastless people.

So we began to divide.

By feeding Bubbles generous amounts of flour and water, I could share two to four cups of starter a day. I discovered a stash of low quality, enriched, bleached flour at my local discount market that would be okay for this process. Not my favorite, but I was begging so I couldn't choose.

I posted a picture of Bubbles on the internet and wrote, "Hey everyone! This is Bubbles, my 100-year-old sourdough starter. If you are looking for a bread-baking adventure with wild yeast, she can give you a good time. Hit me up and I'll hook you up."

And the people showed up with polite requests for a share and instructions.

I fed Bubbles twice a day, and she produced like a champion!

The thing about yeast is that, once you get a happy little colony going and keep feeding it, there's not a lot you can do to stop them. They just keep feeding and multiplying and making new yeasty-beasties and producing the gas that makes all those bubbles.

Yeast and love have a lot in common.

For several days, I gathered little groups in my local supermarket parking lot, doling out small containers to masked people. They would park and call out from behind their doors, "Are you the sourdough lady?" Each container got wiped down with disinfectant wipes before being handed over. We all smiled with our eyes.

I like to think it looked like the world's oddest drug deal.

While Bubbles procreated, I unearthed my feeding, proofing, and baking instructions from the depths of my computer. Written years before when I'd last had a request to share my starter, they now got sent touchlessly via social media message or text. Several of these adventurous bakers immediately zipped back home and jumped into the adventure. Some people even shared images of their new loaves with me.

Bubbles and I showed them off to our friends.

Together, we may not make beautiful loaves, but we do create a lovely harmony.

And our bread tastes delicious.

GETTING FIGGY

The fig tree stood in the corner of my dining room, flopping its gangly branches against the wall.

I was ninety-five percent sure where the smell was coming from.

Despite my mother-in-law's warning, Figgy needed to move outside.

A gift from a friend and her lovely wife as they moved out of Asheville after a short sojourn here, Figgy has had quite a journey for a tree. After keeping her as a houseplant for several years in their home in the Northeast, they moved to North Carolina, where she expanded in the humidity and heat to become a vibrant being. My friends insisted that they wanted her to remain where she was healthiest, so they left her on our deck with a sweet goodbye and a miniature gnome as a guardian.

Figgy stands over six feet tall, with wide, long leaves like you see in those medieval paintings of Adam and Eve. I began researching how to care for fig trees the next day, not wanting to fail her or have to report to them that I'd killed her.

I've killed plants before, through lack of knowledge and bad luck. My green thumb turns black occasionally and, well... Shit, a zucchini died on my watch. A zucchini. The weed squash.

But I knew research could save Figgy!

All of the websites I found recommended putting Figgy in a sunny spot, as long as I didn't leave her outside all winter. At the woodshop where I worked, two fig trees resided on a sunny hillside all year round, and even produced the occasional fruit. Since she lives in a pot and early autumn remained pretty warm, I decided we would leave her outside for a while.

"You should move this tree inside," my mother-in-law pronounced on her first visit. "It shouldn't be in this much sun."

All of the research I'd done on the internet said the opposite. I smiled and thanked her for her advice, planning to ignore it for the rest of Figgy's life.

In the bright sunlight, after being inside for much of her existence, Figgy's leaves began to bleach and dry out. When the first one fell, I panicked. She was right! I was going to kill Figgy!

So I started searching for a place in the house to put her. The dining room held the only space big enough. In a corner next to an east-facing window, the light filtered in through the branches of the maple outside. Ugh. Way too dark. But she'd lived inside for most, if not all, of her life thus far, so she wouldn't mind, right?

With a mixture of lifting and pulling (and our cleaning lady's help), the fig shifted to her new home for the winter. I gazed at the few leaves untouched by white and hoped for the best.

They all fell off.

I kept watering her. She could NOT die! My friends trusted me to keep Figgy alive.

A tiny touch of green at the tip of each branch encouraged me.

Slowly, as fall progressed, leaves reappeared. Small at first, and then growing with abandon.

Figgy lived!

My mother-in-law complimented my good sense on the new addition to the dining room.

Over the winter, we took in a fellow and his cats for a few months while he got back on his feet. The large blank canvas of dirt at the base of the fig tree was too much to resist, and those cats used it as a litter box.

At first, we thought the smell was just the cats having cat wars and marking the room. We sprayed the space down with a natural smell-absorbing spray, which had worked on everything up to this point, but no. Cat piss forever.

Meanwhile, Figgy thrived, unfurling gorgeous, large leaves. Her green branches flailed into the middle of the room. I turned her to brace them upright against the wall. She grew even more unruly.

I cannot explain this away, Figgy! You are a sick, sick girl!

She continued to stink, even after the other cats left.

When the weather warmed to the point beyond frost, I knew what I had to do.

My wife suggested using a piece of cardboard to protect the floor as I slid the planter outside. Figgy rode a flattened box while I grunted and wheezed. She settled just outside our main door on the deck. Again, I spun her around and supported her branches against the house so she wouldn't slump out into the pathway of the deck.

My mother-in-law visited for Sunday dinner. "I don't think this tree will survive outside. It's getting too much sun."

I flinched.

Of course she still disapproved and thought she was right because the tree had thrived all winter. However, everywhere I'd researched, people said the same thing. The tree needed to go into a sunny space. Its limbs had turned weak and leggy from reaching for light.

"The leaves fell off because it was autumn," I replied. "Or because it had been moved. Everywhere I look, they say to put fig trees into a sunny spot. The dining room isn't sunny."

"Okay," she said, in that way that says "At least I warned you" and "You'll be so sad when that tree dies." And then she dropped the subject.

Or so I thought.

Over the next week, the leaves began to turn white and dry, dropping to the deck one by one. Leggy branches drooped into the doorway. Kitchen twine only served to bind them into a big sagging clump of branches and leaves.

But little green tips on the branches promised life, and some of the leaves appeared untouched by white! With each big rain, her kitty perfume washed away a little more.

Each Sunday dinner, the gardening maven mother-in-law tried a new tactic. Last week, the tree wasn't happy outside. Figgy had told her.

Figgy! You traitor!

Leaves continued to drop. What if she was right? What if I killed Figgy with this desperate move to rid myself of the lingering eau de nasty cat?

And then....

As I returned from my morning walks with Mack, I started noticing more and more new leaves forming little umbrellas at the tips of the branches.

Figgy lives!

Here is what I suspected would happen: the old leaves would all fall off. Over the course of the summer, more new leaves would burst from the branches with a dark green fervor, large enough for me to pose as Eve in the garden (and I'm more of a Venus of Willendorf type than the lithe Eve medieval painters portrayed). A judicious pruning would strengthen her limbs. The summer rains and a scrub of the pot's exposed areas would remove the last gasp of the cat spray.

Then at the end of September, Figgy would return to her place in the house, smelling sweet and ready for her long winter's nap.

And you know what? I was right. Which means my mother-in-law was right, too.

That'll teach me.

·❤·❤·❤·❤·❤·

RAINBOW HAIR FIX

At around the sixteen-month mark from my last haircut (Oh. My. Pandemic!), I decided to dye my hair myself.

Before we progress, you should know that my hair is, even in my fifty-first year, naturally brown. Not one gray hair, not even the chin hairs, dammit! My hair DNA descends from my father who, despite a long white beard resembling Santa Claus, reveals still-dark brown hair when he removes his ubiquitous ball cap.

While this blessing, along with that layer of fat that keeps the wrinkles plumped out, makes me appear younger than my age, I lusted for a streak of bright color along the side of my face.

You see, a couple of decades ago, a woman I never met inspired that lust. She walked through a city square in a small town in France, laughing with friends. A streak of hot pink whipped through this woman's otherwise silver hair, and I instantly worshipped her. Who needs purple clothes and red hats when you could have a Pink Streak?! The audacity and brilliance of that mark stamped itself into the soft gray matter of my brain. For the remainder of our trip down the Canal du Midi, we called our barge "The Pink Streak."

I vowed that, when my hair lost its color, I would dye it with the same sort of brilliant colors. Streaks of purple, teal, fuchsia, red, and pink-pink-pink! When I was an old woman, I would dye my hair purple!

In 2018, I was tired of waiting for my hair to turn gray in order to dye it. And, while I may be a cheap-o about most other things, my hair is not one of them. In a carefully scheduled moment of joy, my masterful stylist bleached and then dyed a purple streak in my hair.

I love it. I am in love with that streak of color in my hair. When I look at myself in the mirror, it makes my heart thrum with joy. "Who is that fantastic person with the cheeky purple streak?" I fall in love all over again.

And no amount of ridicule can change my feeling. My boss at the woodshop, NOT a pink-streak sort of woman, tried to ignore it. Giving up on that strategy, she invited a close friend and colleague to visit, who proclaimed it similar to what his sixteen-year-old daughter would do to her hair.

I preened when he left my office, because sixteen-year-old girls give a flying fuck about fashion. Even though the original streak was sighted in France in 1999, my streak still retained its chicness!

My streak alternated between purple and pink and teal. Because these "fashion colors" fade quickly, I kept a backup bottle of purple hair dye to touch up the streak on my own. Every other dying visit, we bleached the brown out of the streak to keep the color bright. Our system kept me a creative bohemian!

But then, the pandemic and the lockdown. I avoided the hair salon, with its possibility of infection, until I could get vaccinated. Through-out the entire germ-ridden time, a pair of sewing shears rid me of my dead ends while my hair grew from darn short to shoulder-length. The brilliant haircut that my stylist bestowed upon me escorted me through the "growing out" wave with grace. While my hair did invade my eye space for a time, there wasn't a moment when it really looked bad. All credit to her for that!

During those sixteen months, my streak faded and descended until only an inch or so of blonde remained. Almost completely brown again, my hair looked at me like I'd lost my damn mind. "Just a little streak!" it would call to me, every time the mirror caught my eye. "You can do it. I know you can."

Hmmmm... Maybe I could.

I studied girls in the grocery store, on the streets, and online like a creepy stalker, following young women who'd obviously bleached and colored their own hair with tremendous results. If they could do it, I could do it. I refused further research and grabbed a box of teal hair dye with associated lightener on my next trip to the drugstore.

That box sat on my shelf for weeks. When I was brushing my teeth after a shower, the ever-so-serious faces of the models taunted me. "What are you afraid of?" their eyes gleamed.

I would pick up the box and put it back down. Saturday will be perfect, I'd think. Lots of time for dying hair on Saturday!

Saturdays came and went.

Fear had me by the split ends.

One of the only things I know is that taking action helps to get me out of that scared place. The next Saturday arrived. I decided to go for it.

My mother taught me to be frugal, and I thought I could mix up just a little bit of the lightener at a time, but that was not to be. I was instructed to mix the whole thing at once. Wasting even one drop seemed so wrong! But I didn't want to dye my whole head. I decided that, in addition to giving myself a bleached little flip on one side, I would give myself another streak on the other side. "How hard could it be?" I told myself. Children do this.

Children also read fashion magazines. Children watch YouTube tutorials.

Children ask for help.

First, how to keep the lightener from bleaching more of my hair than I wanted? When my fabulous stylist bleached and dyed my hair, she would use these thin aluminum foils to isolate small sections.

I could do that! I have aluminum foil!

Using aluminum foil from the kitchen (regular—heavy duty seemed like overkill), I isolated and expanded that little space where my baby flip of a streak remained. I wiped the lightener onto the hair and trapped it, crunching the foil into a ball.

On the opposite side of my head, I grabbed a full section of hair. Wiping on the lightener, I realized I'd grabbed more than I thought. That would be okay though. After all, I wanted a streak. If it was a little wider than I really wanted, well, I could make it work!

I balled the next section of my hair up into the foil. Crumpled aluminum spheres bobbed by my ears, so that I resembled Oscar the Grouch mid-pop out of his trash can. I wandered around the bedroom, feeling proud of my resourcefulness while reading and making tea until the time came to rinse.

But after I cleared the residue of the lightener from my hair, I knew I'd done a bad.

The bleached section with the flip was ok. It wasn't great, and I wouldn't be winning any awards for fantastic styling, but it was basically inoffensive.

A giant bleached spot with odd streaks of blonde dribbled down the other side of my head.

Maybe it would look better after it was dyed.

In the drugstore, the teal dye had glowed from the shelf. When I'd tried it with my stylist before, it had looked fabulous on me. Plus, teal for the spring, right?!

By the time I was done, one half of my head looked like a teenager trying desperately to be cool and the other half like a thirteen-year-old boy who'd gotten shot in the head with a paintball. A giant green spot—a spot! How did I manage that?!—sat squarely in the center of the left side of my head.

A headband pulled my hair back and obscured a direct view of the spot, but I knew I was going to have to 'fess up to my stylist. We had an appointment in two months.

I couldn't hide forever.

Full marks to her. She did not laugh. She merely looked at me and asked, "Do you want to fix it?"

Yes. Oh, yes, I want to fix it. I laughed and said, "Maybe we could do a rainbow stripe for Pride month."

"Really?" she asked, ready to pounce.

"Let's do it!" I couldn't believe my audacity, but why not? I'd been trapped in the house with mouse brown hair that everyone approved of, and then made a detour into a crappy dye job. Let's have a RAIN-BOW!

Over the course of the next several hours, she bleached and painted. I was her compliant canvas.

At the end of our time together, a rainbow draped around my face, with the rest of my head restored to its usual brown. All of the hair stylists gathered before I left, oohing and aahing. The salon took a video and so did my stylist. I was featured on their social media. I felt honored and excited and a little bit famous.

I went home and showed off my new hairdo to all my social media friends. Visiting the office that week, my boss remarked that she was surprised I hadn't ridden my unicorn.

Shows her! My car is my Unicorn. I ride her everywhere! Her name is Honoria.

Everyone says they love my rainbow hair, except my boss at the woodshop, but she's not a rainbow-hair sort of person. She was barely a purple-streak-hair sort of person. All kinds of credit though, because she never invented a dress code and told me I couldn't have purple hair.

The rainbow stripe exactly matched a skein of sock yarn in my stash, which I immediately knitted into a rainbow cuff with red beads to accentuate the little arches of lace.

I gave it to my stylist to remember the rainbow hair by.

I'll use the rest of the skein to make rainbow socks for myself, in a variegated blend of all the colors. Maybe I'll even add beads on the legs. What?! How fabulous will those be?

Stephanie's visit to the salon was the next week and, after I dropped her off, I wandered around downtown to do a little networking. As I walked through the door of a shop, two women stopped talking.

"Oh!" one of them said. "Your hair! When you came through the door with the light shining behind you, you looked like an angel!"

I love being the artwork. Any time an artist uses her paintbrush on me, their love and talent seeps into my skin. Their inspiration transforms me, and I end up beautiful.

Rainbow Up, Folx!

·♥·♥·♥·♥·♥·

MOMMY-DOGGY TIME

S itting in bed on Saturday morning, I look down at Mack, our seven-year-old blue heeler/chihuahua mix. He's twisted into a "c" shape with all four feet in the air, head thrown back, snoring. We call this position "Dog of Pompeii." I pet his belly, and my hand's movement showers dog hair onto the sheets, blankets, pajamas. An unpleasant smell of doggy body odor rises with the disturbance.

There's no avoiding it. It's Mommy-Doggy Time.

A year after we rescued this little lovebug from the pound, the time for Mack's first regular vet checkup arrived. Along with the necessary vaccinations, I needed advice about his belly. He'd licked it red and wouldn't leave it alone. The vet took one look at him and asked when his last bath was.

I couldn't remember. Our Mack-Mack-Dog-of-Love hates bathing, so I didn't force him.

Mama LA got the Vet Smackdown!

After a deworming treatment and an antibiotic shot, the vet sold me a bottle of special shampoo. "Give him a bath with this today and then once every other day until the redness disappears. After that, bathe him once a week with this shampoo to prevent this from happening again."

He followed up the instructions with an especially stern "You can't let your dog run your life" look.

My eyes fell in shame, and Mack caught them with his deep brown gaze of utter devotion. Could I betray those eyes?

Yes. If it meant a better life for him, I would do whatever it took.

Even if he hated me for it.

I straightened my shoulders, lifted my head, and gave the vet a quick nod of acquiescence.

Mommy-Doggy Time began that afternoon.

I used to have a mostly white border collie mix named Cappy. On his daily wanderings, he'd sometimes find the delightful feces of a cow, random wild animal, or another dog. Headfirst dives were the preferred method of ecstatic communion. Coming home, eyes wild with joy and body exhausted from his revelry, Cappy would assault my nose with the smell even before I saw the smears down the sides of his neck and body. His doggy grin never drooped as I'd say, "Oh Cappy! Poopy-dookie!"

With this cue, his paws ran him directly into the shower. After only a couple sessions of learning this command, Cappy got the idea. Poopy-dookie equaled Mommy-Doggy Time! And Mommy-Doggy Time happened in the shower. A delectable refreshment after the rollicking fun!

With all of the shit sprayed off of him by the handheld shower head, I worked cheap shampoo into his thick fur. Little pets convinced him of my love as I scrubbed him clean.

After a final rinse, I'd turn off the shower and command, "Shake it, baby!" His fierce shaking would send the first layer of wetness into a fine spray of mist and dog hair on the walls of the shower. A quick sideways slip out of the enclosure and I grabbed his towel for a final rubbing to wring however much more water I could out of his fur. Once freed, he ended "Mommy-Doggy Time" with a mad dash to roll across every piece of carpet in the house.

With this experience and knowing how much Mack loves the love, I was certain I could get him on board with "Mommy-Doggy Time," despite the fact that he hates water.

Oh yes. Mack hates water. I've never seen a dog who hates water so much. On rainy days, he'll go to the door, asking to go outside. I open the door. It doesn't even have to be actively raining! The water pooling on the deck stops him. His next steps propel him back into the house. "Mack!" I'll say, trying to sound stern. "Go out and do your business."

"No way," his eyes flash as he gives me a look over his shoulder. "I don't have to pee that bad." And he's back to his little nest by the fireplace.

This dog has a bladder of steel!

My only recourse to prevent a bladder infection is to grab the lead and an umbrella. He'll go if I go.

"How about a walk?" I say as I hold the lead aloft. He runs to me, forgetting all about the rain. Walks are his second favorite thing, the first being lying between Stephanie and me on the bed and getting luxurious belly rubs.

The lead clips onto his collar and I open the umbrella as we walk out the door together. He follows, but stays close to me to get the benefit of our protection. He knows I need to see him do both kinds of business, but the pooping usually requires a bit of a walk to make happen. On particularly rainy days, he squats before we even leave the yard.

Returning home, at the edge of our lawn, I remove his lead and he zips up the steps to our front door. "Shelter!" He scratches at the door. "Let me in!" And as soon as the door cracks open, he plunges into the dry house, shaking the moisture from his fur. Tossing me a quick doggy grin, he picks a choice resting spot and cuddles in to dry completely.

A year into regular "Mommy-Doggy Time" sessions, and this is how it goes:

First, like a master spy entrapping her prey, I discreetly close all possible avenues of escape. One of our old towels gets placed near the shower.

As he snoozes, I start the water and wait until it's the warm side of lukewarm. I take off my clothes. He suspects nothing until...

I remove his collar.

His eyes widen. Moving quickly, I scoop all twenty-five pounds of him up into my arms. I begin to sing a jolly song (loosely based on the theme song to the Howdy Doody Show):

It's Mommy-Doggy Time!
Let's get all clean today!
It's Mommy-Doggy Time!
We love getting clean together!

Plop! Into the shower, sliding the doors closed behind me to block his final lunge. With all hope of escape behind him, he freezes into position. His head faces the front right corner and he stands, his body rigid with rebellion as he refuses to look at me.

Water sprays from our handheld shower head, soaking his fur.

I am now the Betrayer, the Traitor, the Bringer of All That is Evil.

I switch from singing to cooing, desperate for redemption. "What a good boy. Scrub-scrub Mack-Mack."

The special shampoo pours into my hand and I suds him up. As we wait for the required ten minutes for the shampoo to do its job, I wash myself and make small talk.

"Oh, he's my good Mack-Mack, good boy. We're having Mommy-Doggy Time. Isn't it fun? It's our special time. What a good Mack boy."

He stands still, staring out of the glass enclosure. What has happened to the good mommy? The one who takes him for walks and showers him with love instead of water? Who is this hell beast and why does she SING and COO while DROWNING HIM?!

My wife comes into the bathroom to pee, and he wills her to open the shower door. His little head droops when she wheels her walker back into the bedroom.

After my own cleansing, I rinse him off and slip out of the shower, closing the door behind me and grabbing his towel. As soon as I re-open the enclosure, he jumps out. The towel immediately drops over his entire body. He submits to drying until I pull the towel off his head. Then he takes off, his shaking progressing from nose to tail before he dives head first into the bedroom carpet. He bounds out of sight to continue his drying process on the hallway runner and finally the den's large rug. Rolling onto his back, he's off to the next location as he erases the lingering evidence of the shower.

I hear him singing his version of our shower song as he races around the house.

Fuck that shower time!
Mommy's a rotten whore!
Oh, fuck that shower time!
I hate it very much!

I don't know where that shitty little asswipe got that nasty mouth, but he's so cute. I can't stay mad. I know I deserve it.

Once his fur dries, I call him. "Mack! Time to put your collar back on."

I hear the scramble of paws across the floor and he's there at my feet, wagging his tail as hard as he can in a perfect sit, ears perked, eyes glancing back and forth between the collar in my hand and my face.

"Oh, my collar! I love my collar! Are you going to put it on me now, Mom?" Wag, wag! Once the collar is back on his neck, he sits up straighter and preens.

The redness on his belly went away entirely in just a few days, and it never returned. Along with the reduction in redness, his shedding decreased by almost seventy-five percent. I'm assuming this has something to do with the regular bathing and also that we stopped feeding him chicken in any form after a friend told me her vet said that quite often dogs can be allergic to chicken. Now, along with the monthly baths, he gets homemade wet dog food made from hamburger, rice, and sweet potatoes. Stephanie even makes a special gravy.

He loves being our dog.

Except for Mommy-Doggy Time.

·♥·♥·♥·♥·♥·

WHAT KIND OF TAPE?

While picking up cat treats at the supermarket, I observed a couple contemplating the tape selection.

"You grab tape and I'll get the dog food," he said and turned to walk toward me. The woman asked, "What kind of tape do you want, Scotch brand or does it matter?" before noticing he'd turned. He continued walking away without answering, distracted by the delectable bags of Purina.

"Oh great. I ask you a question and you just walk away," she said, sighing.

We caught each other's eye, and I smiled. "Of course. He's the only one with an opinion," I remarked as I passed her.

And she immediately began to back up. "No! My opinion counts. I know that."

Oh, Honey. I was racing those barrels while your momma was still teaching you what a horsie was.

"No, no," I laughed. "I didn't mean THAT! I meant that he's the only one who cares about the tape brand. Just like my wife. I could care less about the tape brand–Scotch, generic, whatever–but she has an opinion. Only 3M Blue tape, only Gaffers tape, only matte-finished clear Scotch tape."

"Yes!" she exclaimed. "Oh, yes! Exactly."

"Exactly."

We smiled at each other, and my wife said into my ear, "You know I'm right here. I heard everything you said."

Ever since Covid scurried across the country, our grocery store trips have sent me in person and her in my headphones. My sweetie's voice keeps me company as I work my way through the aisles, asking her about things she wants or whatever comes to mind.

"See you around," I grinned at the woman and continued on my shopping journey.

"Nice to meet you," she called as I turned into the perimeter aisle of the store.

"Everything you said," my darling said again.

"I know. Did I say anything that wasn't true?"

"No."

"Well." I double-checked my basket against my list. "No worries then."

When I was a young housewife, my first grocery shopping trip for the household was a disaster. First I picked up all the regular necessities, and then I began our condiment journey.

Don't you have a condiment journey? Condiments that came to your home to invigorate your cooking and now sit going ever so slowly bad in your refrigerator door because you just know you'll use them again someday? I mean maybe you only use that one to make that amazing Indian dish that you haven't made in years, but why throw away good condiments?

Anyway, I picked up tuna, mayonnaise, blueberries, flour, milk, butter. All the things needed to make dinner and blueberry muffins and tuna sandwiches for lunch. Stocking the refrigerator and the pantry, I rejoiced in the usefulness of my efforts, the way my visiting the grocery store freed my wife to work while I made our household go.

When my dearest love came home for lunch, she opened the refrigerator door and there, on the main shelf, sat the milk, mayo, and blueberries.

My pride radiated from me. I was going to be a terrific housewife, even if I couldn't find a job yet.

And she said, "Miracle Whip?! You got Miracle Whip?!"

Well, shit. I'd done bad. I thought that's what you got when you went to get mayonnaise. Miracle Whip equaled Mayonnaise.

Please don't think less of me. I didn't know the good mayo from the bad then. It wasn't something I ate except mixed into tuna, and I didn't care what type I ever got. The Miracle Whip had been on sale.

The matter quickly got explained to me.

Miracle Whip = Salad Dressing.

Hellmann's = Mayonnaise.

Also, only whole milk and Bumblebee albacore tuna fish and real butter.

The jar of Miracle Whip was dealt with somehow (I can't remember after almost thirty years). My wife shopped with me the next time (I made her come with!), and we worked our way through the store so my knowledge of her preferences could grow into an understanding. From then on, Hellmann's was our house mayo, until we moved to North Carolina, when we changed to Duke's.

All of this is to say that my wife cares about certain brands and types of things and I don't. For many, many years, we only bought Northern Quilted toilet paper, but not the deluxe kind because it's too linty. Then our whole world upended when we realized that Northern was owned by the Koch brothers somehow.

Political boycotts wove into my shopping life early. When I was a child, my mother eliminated everything Nestle from our shopping list to protest its promotion of baby formula in third world countries. I still feel guilty if I find the Nestle brand name on something I bought, even though the boycott ended in 1984.

So, the search began. Since we were switching it up, I thought maybe we could use something substantially cheaper, but with enough heft that we could also use the same roll to blow noses if necessary. Single-ply toilet paper was definitely not substantial enough and felt harsh against my sweetie's patootie. We settled on Angel Soft for a while, but during the pandemic, all of the toilet paper disappeared. We took this opportunity to walk away from toilet paper almost altogether and finally installed the little in-toilet bidet we'd ordered years before. Soft, terry cloth rags took over the job for the most part. However, we do still use a little toilet paper for, you know, sticky situations. The store-brand recycled variety works well. Two-ply, of course. I do think she misses the Northern though.

As I think on it now, I was trained by my childhood to simultaneously care less and more about brands through my mother's search for value. She trained me to look for the first generic labels, plain black writing on white backgrounds. While I happily ate cereal from a bag instead of a box, I rebelled against the generic SpaghettiOs.

They just aren't the same.

The other thing that made me think differently about brands was the inevitable seepage of brand names into our grocery lists. Kleenex for tissue, for example, and in the South, Coke for soda. In fact, when I ventured across the state line from Arkansas into Missouri, I discovered that there was a debate about whether to call it "soda" or "pop." Asked my habit, I admitted we called it "Coke" no matter what the brand or flavor.

That particular practice became a problem when I waitressed at a chain restaurant where they only served Pepsi products. "What would you like to drink?" I would ask.

"Oh, I'll have a coke," the patron would reply, continuing to read the menu.

As trained, I would inform them. "We only have Pepsi. Is that all right?"

This practiced line always confused the patron, who was expecting the traditional, "What kind of coke would you like?"

Sometimes they said yes. Most of the time, they clarified that they would like a 7-Up or Mountain Dew or Dr. Pepper.

Which reminds me of a story my wife likes to tell about visiting Texas for the first time. Going into a Dairy Queen to pick up a drink, she watched the woman in front of her turn to the small band of children to her side and ask, "What kind of coke you want? Dr. Pepper?"

"That's when I knew we'd entered the South," she'll say as she giggles.

For the longest time, I couldn't tell why she thought that was funny. Made perfect sense to me.

And all of this mind meandering almost made me forget the hot dogs after my little chat with Mrs. Still Wondering About the Tape.

I turned back and hurried past the dog food aisle to the cold case. Nathan's were on sale. Hebrew Nationals was our brand forever, but recently I began grabbing Nathan's as well. Ballpark and others I grew up with are off the table.

Buns were around the corner. I grabbed a bag of the store brand. The potato buns are her preference, but the cheapest, squishiest white buns will serve since it can be hard to source the potato ones in hot dog form.

I don't mind these small indulgences. They mean little to our overall life. When one of you has a preference for something, unless there's a pressing financial need, I say, go ahead. Get the thing they want. Or get the thing that you want. It's not about giving your power to the other person. It's about indulging their preference.

And that's ok.

That's the give and take of a normal relationship. That's the "Hey, I got hot dogs for us for lunch one day this week" and having the other person know that you got the good hot dogs. That you got the real mayo and not "salad dressing." That you got red grapes, not the green ones. Whatever the thing is that you take the time to ask "Do you have a preference" about. That's what it is.

What kind of tape do *you* want?

·❤·❤·❤·❤·❤·

MY GARDENING BOYFRIEND

A dahlia bloom gently moves as a bee alights on its petals. The only sound is the bee buzzing and then, with the sudden silence of wings stopping, she begins to collect the nectar.

"Hello. And welcome to Gardener's World." The seductively calm voice spreads across my nerves like honey as the host gives an overview of the coming program.

And that's how Monty Don became my new TV boyfriend.

I don't know if I would have ever started gardening without how-to television shows.

You see, I need a how-to show to get me excited about doing almost any DIY project.

The *Great British Baking Show* propels me into the kitchen for big baking pushes at the holidays. Ree Drummond and Ina Garten turn me on when I've lost the will to make supper. Various fixer-upper shows convince me I can hang pictures and move sofas. Martha Stewart has a lot to answer for with her sensual housekeeping programs!

Good how-to TV inspires me to action, and not always for my own good. Watching *The Dog Whisperer* made me think I could handle a puppy. Two weeks into the relationship, I found myself screaming at the cutest little fluffy puppy in the world as he ran in circles around a huge black bear walking down our street.

A pile of books, one ineffective shock collar, and several different types of leads later, a wonderful dog trainer entered our lives. She showed me how to be buddies rather than "master" and "dog." With her guidance, that cute but obstinate pup turned into one of the best dogs ever.

Never the less, I made my sweetie turn off *Supernanny* as soon as I heard myself think, "Oh yeah. I could be a mom." No way was I going to let that lovely British lady convince me that I could be a mother! If I lost my mind with anger at a cute, fluffy puppy who I already loved soooooo much, what would happen with a child? Best to stick to being an aunt. I'm a really good aunt.

So the evil influence of *Supernanny* got exiled from our television.

Of course, at the beginning, I was unaware of the influence that turned me into a gardener. I'm sure my mother was surprised the first time I put in a garden, encouraged by Eliot Coleman and Barbara Damrosch on *Gardening Naturally*. (They were my first TV threesome.) As a child, I resisted weeding and all sorts of garden chores. All I wanted to do was sit inside and read in the cool air. Pulling weeds meant dirty hands wiping away the sweat pouring into my eyes while mosquitoes buzzed and dove for the parts of my skin where the bug-repelling spray dripped away. The reward of tomatoes and green beans and corn from our own garden didn't seem worth it to my child self. Aaaaah, Arkansas!

Now?! Adding compost and creating beautiful soil, pulling weeds, planting seeds to grow herbs and vegetables and flowers—all of these things infuse me with joy. And sharing that gardening joy with my mother deepens our bond, giving us something to chat about in our weekly phone calls.

In my very first garden in Denver way back in the 90's, I devoted myself to growing tomatoes and herbs. Flowers found their way in, but mostly on the edges. The Coleman-Damrosch influence pushed me to provide four seasons of food for my family, as did the classic *Victory Garden* hosts. Piles of tomatoes and basil tumbled from that first garden, producing caprese salads, a couple of trays of pesto ice cubes, and one pot of tomato sauce that I added meat to and insisted on calling "marinara" until my sister-in-law corrected me.

Years worth of cooking shows still lay in my future.

Over the decades (Geez! I'm an old lady!), *The Victory Garden* kept me excited, though I stopped watching religiously when we moved into the high Rockies and I lost that first summer's green beans to an overnight snow on the Fourth of July.

And then PBS canceled the show.

I won't say it was because I stopped watching but....

The move to North Carolina meant an expansion in my gardening world once again. After nineteen years of a fifty-nine day summer, the 176-day growing season feels luxurious in its expansiveness.

During my very first Appalachian summer, I discovered *The Almanac Gardener*, a PBS North Carolina-produced program run by cooperative extension agents from across the state. Their knowledge supports me in my gardening journey, teaching me what I can grow and the possible pitfalls as I acclimate to this new area.

The bounty of succession planting! The dangers of the giant grass! The bugs upon bugs upon BUGS!

When the pandemic arose, *The Almanac Gardener* went on hiatus, even though I had more time to garden.

Rude!

But understandable.

Dang my forgiving nature!

To make up for the lack of new episodes, I took advantage of the archived seasons on my PBS app. Weeks slipped by as I consumed show after show.

Running out of those, I turned to the other PBS gardening programs. They were good, but I wanted something more. I miss *The
Victory Garden*, you know what I mean? That show made me smile,
and was worth getting up at 7:30am on a Saturday morning to watch.

In my desperation, I turned to *Gardener's World* on BritBox.

And you know what happened there.

Of course, it isn't only Monty Don. Several wonderful expert gar-
deners share their enthusiasm and knowledge. With their guidance,
my fears dissipated. My reluctance to use pots for veggies and tulips
vanished. When friends offer me seeds, I scramble to grab them, scat-
tering them over the surface of dirt-filled plastic trays recycled from
ground meat purchases. Once they get their true leaves, pricked-out
seedlings (doesn't that sound fancy?) are transferred to individual
pots.

Or I can simply plant the seeds in little pots made from discarded
toilet paper rolls, which can then go directly into the ground. DIY for
the W-I-N!

When the various hosts discussed soil composition using words like
compost, vermiculite, and grit, I purchased a bag of potting soil and
began to put my old veggie ends in the compost bin again.

Because of their zest for flowers, a packet of zinnia seeds sits in the
little bag I use to store my seeds from past years. Nasturtiums bloom in
the buckets suspended on the purple pallet that leans against the wall
outside our main door. Sunflowers and cosmos peer out from their
garden homes.

They also got me excited to create a garden where wildlife could
thrive. A place that nurtures bees and butterflies and small mammals.

At least until I found the dead baby bunny in the yard after our
seventeen-year-old cat had a hunting spree. Yuck! The Great Huntress

continues to putter through her retirement, delivering our cucumbers from the predation of one less bunny.

I have plans. A wildflower meadow at the top of our yard might help arrest the erosion that's happening on the steepest sections of the lawn. For the first time since we moved into this house, I trimmed the azaleas to make room for Noah.

Noah is my mother-in-law's elephant ear plant. She named him and shares bits of him each spring with lucky folks. I helped her plant our bit in the flower garden in the heat of a Sunday afternoon. His six-foot-tall plume of three-foot-long leaves will transform our front flower garden into a tropical paradise (if enough people ignore the little lawn of weeds bursting from the red clay below him).

With some people, television shows trap them inside to lie on the couch all day and binge entire series. I use these how-to shows to get me moving. They push me to try new things and make changes in my life. They get me out in the garden, away from the television and into the sunshine.

Oh yes, Monty! Talk to me about gardening!

It's time to turn the compost heap.

·♥· ·♥· ·♥· ·♥· ·♥·

THAT SPECIAL LA FASHION SENSE

When I came out almost thirty years ago, I didn't really know about femme lesbians. Picturing a lesbian in my mind, I saw a boyish woman with short hair wearing a flannel shirt, boots, and a no-nonsense attitude. Probably with a toolbelt.

Rawr. Yummy!

But not me.

So when I first discovered that lesbians wearing dresses wasn't breaking the rules, it felt like freedom! I wasn't confined to that one masculine look.

Which was lucky because the eccentric and elegant ladies from Agatha Christie novel adaptations, Golden Age Hollywood movies, and popular eighties television shows had built my fashion sense. These ladies wear flapper dresses brimming with beads, luxurious evening gowns skimming perfect figures, flowing caftan tops with skinny jeans and high-heeled sandals. Glorious wraps swing around their shoulders to hold back the cool air of the evening. Dainty heels click quickly along marble-floored hallways. A mysterious grace allows them to glide through crowded bars and dinner parties, leaving nothing but amazement in their path.

Being a little woman, sturdy rather than elegant and round where they are lithe, has always been a problem for me, as far as fashion is concerned. One would never describe me as "naturally graceful," though some have called me "clownishly clumsy." Still, I yearn for the dramatic.

A cape thrown around my shoulders adds verve to any entrance, handily catching doorknobs and turning every carefree "Hello!" into a strangled "H-urg." Bright flowy dresses and long tunics over leggings mimic wings, sweeping any poorly placed fragile items to the floor. The weight and sparkle of beaded dresses transform with their sophistication, shedding their beads to leave glittering clues of my presence between your floorboards.

I know you can't wait to invite me to your next gathering!

When I dreamed of growing up to be a creative writer and actress, I thought my wardrobe would include multiple dramatic capes and jaunty berets. My disappointment when that cape didn't appear during my early college years as a theater major caused my mother, an amazing seamstress who loved to indulge her children, to create a gorgeous ankle-length, brown and black plaid wool cape for me.

I wore that cape draped over me and my backpack all autumn and winter, lurching across the campus like Quasimodo. Entrances necessitated an immediate drop of the backpack (Thunk!) and a swirl of the cape (Whoosh!) as I unhooked the collar and removed it from my shoulders.

That cape still hangs in my closet today, reminding me that I can attain that same sophistication again.

Or go carol-singing with a Victorian quartet.

Unfortunately, all of these flowy, sparkly clothes I LOVE make me look so much fatter than I actually am. Today, eighty pounds away from my sort-of-skinny years, jeans and a button-down shirt win the fashion battle for my body type. This combination compresses and skims to slim what can be slimmed. The flowy clothes I love hide the tiny breath of an idea of the hourglass figure I maintain by accident of fate.

If I follow fashion's sense, then people never believe me when I tell them my dress size.

"No!" They say, trying to shove me into a regular XL. "This will fit!" Zippers stick. Buttons strain. A glance into the handy mirror shows a sausage of a woman, corpulence rolling underneath the fabric.

"Nope! I need the 2x," I'll reply, and pull on the same piece in the larger size, which now skims, flattering my shape and slimming me down. "See?"

They see.

Despite knowing my own size better than those who look at me, I am still a big nerd when it comes to fashion. So when I got my last job as an office assistant, my sister-in-law, who has that effortless sense of what looks good on herself (everything) and others (we have to be more careful), took me shopping. She led me through the shops of the local outlet mall, finding pieces and pairing them together into outfits. By the end of the day, I had a new work wardrobe and a feel for what looked best on me. Shirts that skimmed, pants that flattered, and shoes that lifted my heels just the slightest bit.

One blouse that she encouraged me to grab reminded me of shirts worn by plump business ladies, more flowy than skimming, covered in a bright and busy purple and teal pattern with pintucks lining the front. Despite my adoration of flowy, I protested this choice but she insisted. I took it home, feeling like it gave me a fat-lady work casual look that I was trying to avoid. Pairing it with my favorite purple boiled wool blazer reduced the impact somewhat. Despite my reservations, the top looked good on me. However, its appearance remained rare.

As I watched *The Pioneer Woman* the other day, I thought to myself, what cute shirts she always wears! I should get a shirt like that.

I noticed the details and the shaping and suddenly realized.

I have that shirt in my closet.

And I've been avoiding wearing it.

I resolved to pull out that patterned shirt and begin wearing it as soon as the weather turns.

Maybe I'll even go back to the outlet mall and find more of them.

My sister-in-law really does know what I should be wearing!

And that's lucky for me since today's loosening of the fashion laws mean that people of all genders and sexualities and ages can wear whatever they want, whether they are butch or femme or other. Every dive into my wardrobe means a new identity can emerge for the day, and no one will think twice about it.

Watch out for my cape!

·♥·♥·♥·♥·♥·

MADEMOISELLE DARLING GIRLFRIEND SWEATER

For those of you who don't know, I love to knit. For a few years, this passion bloomed into an obsession, causing me to become a professional knitter.

What the heck does a professional knitter do? I mean, besides take a vow of poverty?

Well, I designed and edited knitting patterns, taught knitting classes, wrote articles about knitting, and even became a partner in a yarn shop. All that ended several years ago when tendonitis in my arms curtailed my knitting.

I used to knit ALL. THE. TIME. And when I say all the time, I knitted a sweater for myself in nine days once.

Nine days.

For myself.

And I'm not a skinny person.

Those days of knitting for three, six, nine hours at a time are done.

Okay, so there have been the occasional twelve-hour marathons, but that was when I was knitting to a deadline, like test-knitting patterns or knitting up the class sample.

Now, I split my knitting time into thirty-minute chunks at the most, resting my hands after each session.

Back in March, I began knitting a wedding gift for my niece and, to give my hands their necessary rest and variation in needle size (because that helps too), I also started a sweater.

This sweater came to me in a dream a couple of years ago. She's knitted from this mostly magenta, variegated yarn using a stitch called the mistake rib. When blocked, this loose rib turns the worsted-weight merino into a soft, snuggly, light cloth perfect for cold Appalachian winter evenings. A sweater to throw on after a long day of work. A sweater for weekend hikes or a movie night in front of the fireplace.

You should see it! It's so cute! And innovative! I'm leaving the sides open (what?! So cool!). The long, closely fit sleeves start just above the elbows. Very flowy, with size based on the length between my elbows when my arms are outstretched.

Kind of like a poncho with arms.

But cute.

My ability to knit these days depends on my not overdoing it in the garden and regular visits to my chiropractor.

A grueling session of pruning the hedge in August left all my knitting projects idle for a couple of weeks. My hands itch to get back to the needles, and I've been testing my fingers with a few stitches on occasional evenings with the wedding knitting.

The sweater started to get jealous.

During my Kaizen-Muse Creativity Coaching class one evening, the sweater pushed its way into my mind during a guided relaxation. She named herself the "Mademoiselle Darling Girlfriend Sweater."

Good Lord. Even my whimsical mind thinks that might be a little much.

Then last night, when I picked up the wedding gift to work on it, I noticed that her project bag had moved onto the coffee table. I'm sure

I dropped her there during the scramble when I spilled water a couple of days ago. Still, spooky! As she sat there with her yarn spilling out of the bag, she taunted me. "Don't you want to knit me instead?"

"No! I'm not even at the halfway point. I need to knit the wedding gift or it will never be done in time!"

"Aren't you chilly? Don't you need me more? You should have a new fall sweater."

Her seduction overwhelmed me. I SHOULD have a new fall sweater. I snatched her project bag from the coffee table and knitted a row before commonsense returned.

She's a sneaky one!

Most of my knitting designs come to me like this. They push their way in and I can't escape them.

Two years ago, I finished knitting my favorite rainbow cardigan in the early spring. Her form had arrived in mid-summer the year before, during those days when wool should only be on sheep. But there she was, a rainbow that tumbled out of my yarn cubbies one Saturday morning. I sketched a quick picture, did my figures (did you know that there's LOTS of math in knitting?) and cast on in the cool air of a rainy morning. Over the next nine months, I worked her top down so I could try her on and get her the right length. Her three-quarter length sleeves are perfect for keeping me cozy on the North Carolina winter nights, staying out of the way as I stoke the fire and do the evening dishes. Her warmth comes from a combination of wool and silk. A couple of pockets carry pens and notes, and keep my hands warm for quick trips outside.

Leftovers from her ended up as a matching cowl, hat, and mitten set that sits on top of my coat rack.

I'm beginning to think that Rainbow is my favorite color.

But back to the new sweater. I'm knitting her flat in two big squares, which will be seamed at the shoulder. Decisions about the neck detail still need to be made. With a name like "Mademoiselle Darling Girlfriend," maybe a cowl or an offset collar would work. Still, I may just finish that edge with a little i-cord and leave it at that.

No! No more work on the sweater! I must finish the wedding gift! Maybe just a row.

WHO'S THE CHAINSAW-WIELDING DEMON NOW?

At college, the professor in charge of the theatrical shop, where we theater majors were required to work three days a week building the sets and sewing the costumes for the current production, gave us a "Tour de Death" around the workshop at the beginning of term. Most of the directions ended with, "And don't do it wrong because you could lose a finger or hand or limb and die a bloody horrific death and the university will shut down the shop and we'll all have to find new jobs and theater as we know it will end. Bandaids are in the first aid kit on the wall."

And thus, a terror of power tools rang through me like that first crash of the organ in Phantom of the Opera.

Because of that fear, I refused to use any of the power saws and barely agreed to touch a drill. Since I was really bad at building, I ran a lot of errands. The head of the department and I used to joke that together, we added up to one good worker.

For years after I graduated, this fear never challenged me.

And then we moved to North Carolina, where pruning emerged as a regular part of our gardening.

My power saw adventures started when I realized I couldn't allow the continued obstruction of my front flower garden by brambles of wild blackberries and random weed trees, which emerge like ants from any piece of ignored dirt. Green leaves battered the small window over the sink in our kitchen, and sunlight had to fight its way to the larger window I used for spying on our neighbors.

Soon my view would be completely blocked.

I armed myself with long sleeves, thick gloves, and my pruning shears. While most of the branches could be cleared manually, I quickly realized that several of the saplings required...

The chainsaw.

Gah!

Did you know that chainsaws were invented to assist in childbirth?! Yes, it is a NIGHTMARE! So when we end up running together from that chainsaw-wielding demon in our shared dream, we'll fight him together, right? Or are you faster than me?

Our chainsaw is a petite cordless number, with a power level that most of the craftsmen in my life would laugh at.

Apprehension riveted my eyes to the blade as my wife explained how to use it.

"Do you know where the chainsaw oil is?"

Gulp. "Yes." I'd stored it safely for her use. HER use.

"Good. You'll need to fill the little reservoir. When you want to oil the chain, just hit this button and run the saw for a moment. That will oil the blade."

Oh God.

"You have to hold this other button down for the saw to run."

That's nice. A little touch of safety to spice things up!

I filled the reservoir, pulled on my gardening gloves, and headed out to confront the forest that now filled our front garden.

Several small trees crowded the azaleas and the holly tree that bookend our little flower plot. I started with the one next to the azaleas. That way when the chainsaw's power pulled my arms into a wildly slashing mistake, only a few leaves, maybe a branch, would suffer.

I didn't want to cut down the holly by accident.

With my abundance of caution and the low power of the machine, I was able to control the cuts. The machine wasn't that hard to manage, and it made my work so much easier.

Well, color me happy and hang biscuits from my ears!

For the next hour, little trees fell. Exhausted, I returned to the house and collapsed on the sofa.

I was content. I'd conquered my fear of the chainsaw.

But the nightmare didn't end.

This year, our holly hedge became a roadway hazard.

Now, I've been avoiding dealing with the hedge for the same reason I allowed those trees to overtake my garden plot. While chainsaws suggested the kind of danger found in horror movies, hedge trimmers went a step further and combined my fear of power tools with my fear of water.

How?

Haven't you ever noticed that hedge trimmers look like one of those crazy sawfish? The ones with the long serrated noses?

You know the fish came first. You know some imaginative asshole was out swimming and saw one of those things and thought, "Hey! I could use that to prune my hedge!"

What kind of animal are you?!

A human animal. It's totally a human thing to say.

Following a near collision with the mail truck, I knew the hedge had to be subdued. The branches there are all pretty small, so I told myself my pruning shears could conquer the tangle. A few afternoons of snip-snip-snip and all would be well!

However it turns out that fifty feet of rarely managed hedge needs more than a little snip here and there. After only fifteen, I indulged in several acetaminophen to relieve the pain in my hands and refrained from knitting for a week. When my sweetie received a notice about a hedge trimmer sale, I marched off to the hardware store to confront the aisle of abominations.

The machine from the sale brochure wasn't even stocked (Yay for big box stores!), but I found a cordless one that seemed comparable. A quick swipe of my credit card, and it had a new home.

Making the purchase was all I could manage that day. Charging the battery gave me a respite until my bravery could recharge as well.

My darling told me to spray the blades with WD-40 to lubricate them. The safety mechanism was the same as for the chainsaw, and the familiarity soothed me. With a couple of experimental pulls of the trigger, I happily realized it didn't jump away from me.

I walked up to the bushes and began to cut. The electric motor whirred and the blades chattered as they zipped through the smaller branches. The trimmer purported to cut branches as large as a half-inch, and I tested that to find that they took a little more time, but the trimmer held and so did my hands. In half the time I'd spent trimming manually, I finished what remained.

Confronting the fear of power tools is something I run into all over the place. Maybe it's compounded by the idea that I should be so self-sufficient that I don't even need power tools? Maybe it's just the leftover, remembered feeling of a power tool leaping and chugging and getting away from me.

Or maybe it's a memory from another life, one that helped me decide not to have children.

Keep those chainsaws away from my hoo-ha!

·♥·♥·♥·♥·♥·

GARLIC IS MAGIC

G arlic is magic.

Think about it. Garlic tastes great, repels pesky insects, and heals the sick. With a handy clove of garlic, you can ward off evil spirits, even making vampires recoil! "Ve vant to suck your blood! Unless you've been into the pesto. Gross! Goodbye and good luck!"

See? Magic.

Even the process of growing garlic feels mystical.

When we moved across the country to North Carolina, a friend gave us a bulb of her county-fair-prize-winning garlic. A whole beautiful bulb of garlic with cloves the size of baby fists. In her no-nonsense voice, she instructed us to plant the garlic during the new moon after the first frost.

Plant the garlic during the dark of the moon? What am I, a gnarly old witch?

But I persisted in following her mysterious instructions.

We arrived in North Carolina mid-October. The next new moon fell on October 30th, and I dutifully toddled out on Halloween Eve to plant the garlic cloves behind my mother-in-law's home. (We lived there for a couple of months while we searched for a house.) In a little space where she wouldn't really see them and the lawn mowers for her housing association wouldn't bother them, I dug a few holes and dropped the cloves in with a blessing of encouragement.

Over the next summer, we created beautiful raised beds at our new home. I tended the garlic as well as I could from a distance, and received four bulbs for my trouble. None for eating! I planted all of the new cloves and waited.

Through the following years, our garlic production increased. Last year, we weren't able to use it all, but part of that was due to my honey-bunny preferring to use minced garlic from jars rather than chop it herself. With all of our beautiful garlic available!! However, such are the necessities when a low-energy-day ambushes you.

This year, ten pounds of garlic fill our harvest basket, and my wife plans to freeze some in tablespoon-sized balls. That will keep us away from those little jars!

Right now, we're in the time of October's new moon, but the weather is still temperate. Warm and wet with rain dripping out of the sky and onto our skylight. Only the turning leaves remind me that winter is coming.

So I wait for the next new moon on November 4th to plant.

And then the magic moves underground. A transformation occurs with no more action from me until next July when I harvest pounds of fresh full bulbs.

At that point, the garlic moves into our dining room.

You see, garlic needs to dry out for a while after it's been harvested so it stores longer. To do this, the garlic bulbs must be spread out and left to their own devices in a cool, dry space. That process is called "hardening off."

Here, the only place I can count on to be dry is in our house. And we hardly ever use the dining room.

Thus, the house fills with the smell of fresh garlic for a few weeks.

We like it, but some people wrinkle their noses with revulsion.

I suspect they are vampires, but my sweetie says it's not nice to make those sorts of assumptions.

Just kidding! She agrees with me.

As the garlic finishes hardening off, the smell recedes.

Then I brush the remaining dirt away, trim the neck and roots, and store the bulbs in a handy basket. This year, it's an Easter basket that my wonderful darling received about a decade ago from some hacker guy in Russia who decided he loved her.

What? Like I'm going to waste a nice basket?

With all of the garlic processed, I pick the largest, healthiest-looking bulbs and set them aside for planting.

As I put my garden to bed each fall, clearing worn-out plants and harvesting any remaining herbs, one plot prepares for new planting. Compost folds into the top layer of dirt, and then I poke the cloves into the cool earth. Later in the autumn evening, the remains of the deceased vegetation burns in our fire pit.

Time to ditch the duds and dance around the fire!

Yep. I'm a gnarly old witch.

I blame it on the garlic.

SILLY STROKE STORIES

To catch up anyone who doesn't know, my wife had a stroke back in 2017, which left her with impaired mobility. While having a stroke isn't very funny, moments do show up, and humor helps me stay calm.

And, in my defense, who could resist giggling just a little at a woman writhing on the floor insisting that nothing was wrong when she was obviously unable to rise on her own?

Most of you?

Oh. Well done.

In the immediate aftermath, my wife traveled from the hospital to rehab, and I navigated being in our new North Carolina home alone each night. Most of my days were spent at her side in the rehab center. Sharing silly stories along with the updates on her condition on social media kept my creativity engaged and my sanity intact.

Things you need to know for these stories:

Ty was our small blonde terrier, seventeen pounds of lovebug and attitude. My mother-in-law babysat her each day while I spent time at the hospital and rehab facility.

Asiago was a hefty fluffy orange tabby and the brother of our Great Huntress, Dolce.

Mack didn't join our household until 2019, so he's not in the stories. However, he did insist on being mentioned here, since I will be mentioning the other pets. Here you go, buddy!

9/23/17

BREAKING NEWS: My wife invented new exercises to practice controlling her left hand.

SILLY STORY: As has become typical on the way home from the hospital, I stopped by my mother-in-law's to pick up Ty, grabbed a comforting box of McNuggets (no judging! I'm in distress), and then drove home in the dark.

As I opened the car door, Ty pushed by me and dove into the darkness. It's the usual pattern. She'll run about and have a good unrestricted poo in the yard before bounding back into the house.

The cats zipped between my feet as I walked through the doorway, leaving the door wide open to give the pets unfettered access. Unwilling to venture too far from the coming supper, the kitties hung out on the deck.

I grabbed cans and spoons and dry food to construct all the pets' dinners. Ty appeared by her food bowl.

Out of the corner of my eye, I saw Dolce, the tortoiseshell kitty, crouched by the counter, her eyes focused on something I couldn't see. For sure, a mouse. She'd brought a mouse into the house. That was the last thing I needed.

I leaned in to save the poor thing and six bajillion legs attached to a stick body FLEW up at me! FLEW! The damn thing was at least six inches long.

"GAH!" I stumbled back and began to yell, "BIG BUG! BIG BUG! Get out of my house!" The cats pursued their prey through the kitchen, trapping it between the refrigerator and a cabinet. Thwarted, they returned to the deck.

"BIG BUG! BIG BUG! Get out of my house!" I ran for a kitchen towel.

"BIG BUG! BIG BUG! Get out of my house!" I flung the towel into the space and dragged the bug across the floor, continuously screaming my new mantra, finally flinging it through the door onto the deck in between the kitties.

Both cats began to advance upon the wriggling beastie in the towel.

SLAM.

Whew.

But...No! Forget it. The towel would be retrieved later.

Now, dinner for the cats and the dog.

When I finally opened the door again, the kitties ran inside to their food bowls, clearly bored with the lackluster entertainment. The bug still lay entangled in the towel. With everything in my being screaming my now favorite phrase, I used as few fingers as possible to pick up the towel and fling the bug off the deck into the darkness.

Ew. Just ew.

My wife and I have a deal: I handle all of the animal effluvium; she disposes of the bugs and mice and dead beings.

Now, I have to manage all of it.

I hate this new deal!

9/25/17

BREAKING NEWS: My sweetie typed today and even managed to get at least a few words spelled correctly.

Well, it's hard when your left hand isn't cooperating.

SILLY STORY: Ty, Dolce, and Asiago took over the bed, pushing me into the center and trapping me exactly where they wanted me.

I surrendered.

I'm blaming the exhaustion. At least I still have a few little beings to snuggle at bedtime.

9/26/17

BREAKING NEWS: My darling's stuck in the Big House–I mean, the rehab center–for at least another week.

SILLY STORY: Her new roommate moved in on Friday. She's a 91-year-old actress with dementia. Georgia started off a little weird, but in a good way. As I left the room on her first night, I asked what she was doing.

"Misbehaving."

Heeheehee.

The next day, she got a little hostile towards my wife. As my sweetie tried to clarify something for the nurse trying to figure out an issue Georgia was experiencing, Georgia's inner diva came out and yelled, "Shut it! She's talking to me."

Well then.

I giggled. My honey sighed, rolled her eyes, and shut her mouth like any smart member of the stage crew.

Later, another CNA asked Georgia what was wrong. "I hate my roommate."

"What? She's such a nice lady."

"She's a woman?!"

This was definitely headed in the wrong direction!

Today, as we rolled back through the door after group therapy, she asked my dearest love, "Who are you?"

"Your roommate."

A completely unimpressed "Oh" dripped from her lips.

10/17/17

BREAKING NEWS: On Thursday, my wife gets to come home. It feels like "FINALLY!" but the PT told us that, with the severity of her symptoms when she arrived, this month in rehab has actually been lightning fast.

She's always been an overachiever.

SILLY STORY: A couple of weeks ago, I sat on the patio at the facility, reading and refreshing myself on my sweater knowledge before the workshop I was teaching. A motion caught my eye, and I looked up to see a sea of wheelchairs rolling down the driveway.

Motors buzzing, the riders moved as a group, driving to the end and then hauling ass back. They appeared to be students, learning what it takes to drive one of these motorized wheelchairs so they could teach their patients in the future.

Laughter and then a couple of startled yelps pealed from the pod as people drove their wheelchairs off-road onto the grass beside the drive.

Hope they wore their seat belts!

10/19/17

BREAKING NEWS: My honey-bunny, sweet love, hero of my heart is HOME!!!!!!

SILLY STORY: On her final evening, my wife relaxed with a cup of coffee. Her last roommate's voice carved a gravel road through the curtain, asking what she was drinking.

"Coffee. Do you like coffee?"

"No," she grated back. "I only drink coffee when I'm in jail."

***

I'm glad I wrote those silly stories because the ones that hang in my head are more about the awfulness than these little moments of mirth that made the days bearable.

Joy and silliness and whimsy and humor heal us in our dark moments. A compliment on the sidewalk from a stranger as you pass them. A witty protest sign. A flower in the barrel of a gun.

I'm sure that in the future I'll share the stories of how I terrorized the nurses and confronted the doctors, but today I celebrate the silly.

Take a moment and notice your joy.

You can thank me later.

·♥·♥·♥·♥·♥·

THE QUEEN OF THE WORLD REPLACES THE FAUCET

On a recent Saturday morning, my normal teapot of Earl Gray called to me. With water kettle in hand, I grabbed the handle of the kitchen faucet.

POP!

The handle, a four-inch-long thin bar with a now-corroded end, rested in my hand as water poured from the faucet! Gah!

I filled the kettle, because sometimes I think quickly, and then inserted the little handle back into the tilting part that actually switched the water off and on. I levered it carefully into place to stop the flow and left the handle balanced in the hole.

Time to replace the kitchen faucet.

Shit.

I'd avoided the task for weeks, shepherding this one through hospice while my wife spoke encouraging words about the new faucet she'd ordered. Chrome peeked from the cardboard box, trying to intrigue me with its double nozzles, one for the simple stream of water and the other to spray. We like a more industrial look to our kitchen faucets, and this one could slide right into service in the back of a small restaurant.

Resigned to today's new task, I picked the instruction booklet up off the coffee table (my smart sweetie left it in a convenient place to aid the new faucet in its seduction) and went back to the bedroom to tell her the good news.

With wrenches and a special tool for installation, I approached the old faucet. My phone's flashlight illuminated my workspace and lay conveniently out of my way. Underneath, the main water inputs turned off with a twist of little knobs on the pipes. Then I lowered myself down, turned onto my back, and gingerly eased myself into place under the connection. With two adjustable wrenches, one to hold steady and the other to unscrew, I released the first of the old faucet's connectors, which spat little dribbles of water into my face.

"Oog!" I spluttered and shot out of the space, scrambling for a bucket. Poised anew with the bucket carefully placed to catch the water, I unhooked the second pipe, which spun and caught me again before I could aim it at the bucket. A couple of drips found their way inside.

Time to disconnect the old faucet from the sink! The special installation tool to loosen and tighten the large nut that keeps the faucet on the sink is sturdy red plastic. A deep channel runs through the handle so the hoses that connect to the water can run through the middle. The end fits the nut exactly, and has little tabs that slide into slots on the handle to hold it in place. It's bright red for no reason at all. You run the little hoses through the short piece and then slot the handle onto the smaller piece. With this leverage, you screw or unscrew the nut.

With the special wrench in place, I hauled on the handle, hoping my strength would move the nut, and heard the faucet hit the wall. "Honey? Can you hold the faucet in place?"

"Yes!" Sitting far away from the handyperson action had been almost physically painful for her. I knew that, but needed to figure these things out on my own. With her guidance. But with my figuring. The wheels of her walker rolled across the floor toward me. "I didn't want to get in your way."

"Thank you." I meant it. Her fingers itch with knowledge, but their loss of dexterity means that I have to perform the task. Her frustration floods through the process as she tells me how she would do things. Combined with my inability to do these processes in exactly the same way, my irritation overwhelms the dam of my control.

I've always been a passenger-seat person. I can drive, but I'm so happy in the passenger seat, knitting and singing and navigating and playing with the radio dial. After the stroke, I moved to the driver's side forever. A big part of that is learning how to do simple household repairs. Change out the faucet. Replace the flapper thingy in the toilet. Figure out why the bidet is leaking.

So, we dance as I fix things. With the flapper thingy, I had to tell her to get out of my way. To leave me be as I figured out how *my* hands perform these tasks. How they work and what they do as I navigate these repairs. Tell me what she knows and then let me fail so I learn.

Hopefully without leaks or odd squeaks or art dropping off the walls.

It wasn't the right place for that painting, anyway.

So now my handy darling rolled into the kitchen. With her holding the faucet, I leaned backward under the sink and turned the wrench below, unscrewing the nut. One more splash of water across my face and the faucet was out! My wife held it up like a trophy.

"You did it!" She grinned. "Now to put the other one in."

Right.

The area which had been hidden under the escutcheon cleaned easily. Thank goodness since that escutcheon refused to be parted from our ex-faucet. Both sank into the garbage can with my thanks for their years of service.

We needed to put the new faucet in the old hole (hey now!) and make sure I could see how everything fit together before we sealed it. The faucet fit well, but when I stretched the hoses over to the water pipes, I noticed that the input of the pipes was wider than the hoses.

Dammit.

I gave my dearest love the news.

"They make adapters. Take the pieces and go to the hardware store. Not Lowe's. Go to Ace. Someone there will actually help you."

And so I was off in the car, making my trip to the helpful hardware store to get supplies.

Local hardware stores are like local bookstores. Every town needs one. They are the places where the people who love making home repairs and painting and all of the other things live, and where you can find someone to actually help you find those things that can adapt your hose to your coupler. I think that's what it's called. If it's not, that's my name for it now.

A Very Nice Young Man used my faucet (which had the hoses attached) and the coupler to find two more pieces which helped me to make the change from the wide end to the skinnier hose. I bought two sets and some teflon tape to make the connections solid.

At home, I screwed the adapters together while standing at the cutting board in the kitchen. Putting teflon tape on the connections helps to prevent leaks. This particular type of tape holds to the surface through tension instead of stickiness, so it must be applied with assurance.

Also, the tape must wrap around the screw part in the direction that I would be twisting the nut onto it. Figuring out which direction would help me achieve the desired "Righty-Tighty" (You know,

Righty-Tighty, Lefty-Loosey?) took a bit of time. And I wanted to do as much of it outside of the undersink cabinet as possible. As with most plumbing projects, there's a bit of odd body placement involved, and this cabinet bites me right in the love handles!

With all of the adapters connected to the couplers, I now needed to put the new faucet onto the sink. My favorite handy-lady came back over to help. She applied a generous amount of clear silicone caulk to the edge of the hole to seal the edges of the faucet and prevent water from leaking into the cabinet underneath. Then, with all of the proper gaskets in place, she slid it into its new home. While she held steady, I leveraged myself under the sink again (Hey, no hickies, you cheeky thing!) and used the same weird red plastic tool to screw the big nut and associated gasket into place. With that done, I lifted myself up to give my back a break and behold the faucet. Beautiful!

Back underneath, the same two adjustable wrenches joined the faucet hoses to the appropriate input pipes. Everything felt nice and solid.

I turned on the water.

And, while the connections held, water beaded at the joints.

Dammit!

I tightened and tightened and tightened, then finally just wiped them with a towel. Overnight, the pipes would dry fully and reveal the exact placement of the leak. After all, with four connections, the choices abound!

A simple slide and click attached the sprayer to the faucet. We tested to make sure the hot came out of the hot side and the cold out of the cold. It did! Yay me!

I relaxed on the couch for the rest of the day.

The next morning, I couldn't resist diving back underneath the sink first thing. Yep. Still a little leak. I tightened some more.

Over the week, the leak turned into more of a seep, but I'm going to have to undo one connection and apply more teflon tape. Dammit!

When I complete these small household repairs, I know I am THE QUEEN OF THE WORLD! Actually, projects aren't officially finished until I yawp out those words and swing my fists into the air, prancing around the room in a daze of glory.

For now, I guess it's time to dig out the teflon tape. Or pipe dope. Or plumber's putty. Or whatever mysterious ichor prevents leaks.

sigh

The Queen of the World hates plumbing.

·❤· ❤· ❤·❤·❤·

STINKY, STANK, STUNK

On the day menopause finally let me know that all of my eggs were GONE, I DANCED! Oh happy day! A joyous toss of the remaining sanitary napkins into the trash can. Or rather, a joyous gift to another home where they are needed. Lesbian Law #2: Reduce, reuse, recycle!

When my wife was forced into menopause by surgery back in 2005, I purchased THE book. Just like mothers give their daughters copies of *Are You There God? It's Me, Margaret* as their cycles begin, women who've traveled through menopause recommend copies of Susan Weed's *Menopausal Years: The Wise Woman Way*. Aqua letters cool the bright fuschia cover. Open and find yourself in a spiritual, physical, and emotional reading of menopause. What problem are you having? She covers most of them. Delve in for your answer.

Namaste.

Blessed Be.

Amen.

However...

While I have a respect for the deep magic that lives within us, when I read sentences like, "Your egg basket empties. Your memory basket becomes heavier," I want to throw the book across the room and scream, "SHUT UP, YA FRUIT LOOP!" I want that book to hit the wall, or better yet, the fireplace, and burst into a million flaming stars.

And then, ten minutes later, I grab the book from the table where I dropped it in disgust and flip to the pages that detail the issue of unexpected rage.

My biggest surprise with menopause was stinky armpits. I mean "dead skunk on the side of the road in the summer that makes you check and make sure no skunk is actually in your car" stinky.

The smell emerged within about five minutes of putting on deodorant. I didn't just stink. I was shower-fresh and STAAANKY!

Susan Weed has nothing to say about the STANK.

Recently, I read a book by Mary Roach called *Grunt*, all about the science of the military. Not the shoot-em-up weapon science, but the science of sleep and smell and pressure and surgery. The nerdy part of military life. At one point, she writes about an OSS plot to turn enemy allies against each other by making them think the other smelled bad. Within the litany of bad smells tested, one was described as "onion-garlic-hoagie." What the what?! I ran to tell my sweetie. "Look! That's me! That's my armpit smell!"

"What? Oh yes. That's it. Yay, you."

My armpit smell gained me the inglorious nickname in our household of "OP," which stands for Onion Pits. Mack the Dog cuddles up close when OP emerges. I stay at least six feet away from anyone else and clamp my arms to my sides.

So, with my new stronger-than-any-deodorant scent, what was I going to do? Luckily, because of the pandemic, I worked from home, and when I went out, my STANK got dulled by everyone else's masks.

If they were wearing them.

WEAR MASKS, PEOPLE! The nose you save may be your own.

But the masks and working from home would only last so long. Eventually, the pandemic would end and we'd all come out of our homes and I WOULD STILL BE STINKY.

Unless the STANK dissipated after the hormones finally retreated? Please!!!

My menopause guru had nothing to say about how long that retreat would take. Some shit about being in the space and wouldn't it be nice to be able to go away from the world for a few YEARS as our crone self emerged?

YES IT WOULD!

FYI - the surprise rage intensifies the STANK. As do the hot flashes and my short workouts and dog walks.

I changed deodorants, cycling through many different options. No dice.

As hot flashes made it uncomfortable for me to be inside my skin, I focused on them. Maybe the solution for those would alleviate the STANK.

While sipping raspberry leaf tea, I read an email from a friend who had success in her hot flash battle by getting rid of certain pieces of her diet: sugar, wheat, caffeine, liquor. When she recommends this diet, she says most people look at her like she's suggested eating a baby.

At this point, I was willing to be a cannibal.

As I'd cut way back on my drinking months before, that was easy. My main sugar intake changed from processed sugar to more natural forms like honey and maple syrup and fruit. Wheat and caffeine took more effort, but I did manage to cut way back on consumption.

My modified "Eating Babies" diet got rid of the majority of my hot flashes, and the cooler weather made them more bearable.

The STANK though. None of these dietary adjustments alleviated the smell that would drive the demons back to hell.

And that's when my darling mentioned a new product to me. Lume. Pronounced Loo-mee.

This glorious bit of genius. This masterpiece of chemistry. This nose-saving cream.

First, this cream–because it's a cream and not a bar or a wet roll-on–this cream can be rubbed anywhere on your body where you have a smell you don't like. I don't know how it works, but that smell just disappears. The packaging says it lasts for 72 hours, but I've found that my onion pit funk can get through in about thirty. Which is much better than five minutes.

With this new miracle odor decreaser, I wear sundresses and sleeveless shirts without the worry of killing any small animals who come near. I mean, I love how Mack the Dog cuddled no matter what, but I was concerned he was inhaling too much of that poisonous odor.

Finding this one product relieved me of so much embarrassment and discomfort.

Now to find something that helps the rage. Where did I put that book?

Oh right! Thank goodness it's still too warm to light a fire.

·❤·❤·❤·❤·❤·

Finally Organized

We always have a room that is packed to the brim with stuff. Boxes to unpack, extra pieces of furniture, art to be hung, office supplies. Kind of like a junk drawer, but an entire room.

In our current home, that was the guest room with a bit of leakage into the library/living room area. However, by the third year of living here, I managed to compress all of these extras almost out of sight in the guest room closet and behind the sofa in the living room.

Never say I'm not resourceful.

Then, at the end of 2020, we invited a fellow to take shelter with us. He and his cats were having a hard time finding a place to live, but he appeared to only need a little bit of a hand-up and he'd be on his way to a successful life.

Thus, I transported the mountain of clutter from our "Fibber McGee" guest room closet to the middle of the library/living room, a place we don't use often but which I have to pass through each day to get to my office.

In order to clear out the clutter, relocate my wife's tools from the tent garage that barely protected them, and give this fellow a place to park his scooter that was lockable, we purchased a "shed in a box" from one of those big box hardware stores on the promise of it getting constructed by this same fellow.

Ten months later, we still had a shed lying by our front door in rotting cardboard boxes, the fellow having not been a great choice for this endeavor due to the fact that he remained high all day and could not be trusted with power tools.

So much for that great career as a handyman!

Also, he left as soon as we got the concrete pad poured for the foundation.

In September, my old woodshop began a search for a place to house a new craftsman moving to the area. This Nice Young Man appeared focused and energetic, ready to pursue his career of being a wood-worker. He just needed a temporary place to stay until he could find his own rental in the super-competitive housing market of Asheville.

After the nightmare of the feckless handyman, I resisted but then gave in. Yes. The Nice Young Man could come and stay with us. After all, it was only for a few weeks. He'd find his new home soon enough.

The earnest look of a Nice Young Man inquiring into my needs with a ma'am tacked onto the end turns me into a pile of pudding! Not in a sexual way, but rather a "let me pinch your cheeks and feed you cookies" way. That precious question makes me want to ask him to pluck items from high shelves, lift heavy boxes, and open doors for me.

Oh, Thank You!

One of the first mornings after he moved in, he asked if there was anything he could do for us. We mentioned the shed, and he spent his second weekend in our home constructing it.

Yeah, baby!

He didn't eat sugar (I know, right?!), but I made a big pot of chili.

Once the shed was up, I began moving our items around like I was working a giant one of those puzzles with the squares that make a picture, but one of the squares is missing. You know the ones that you have to slide the squares around and usually end up with one piece still out of place and you throw it across the room in frustration. And then some random person comes along and finishes it like it's easy. Zip-zip-zip! All done!

You know what I'm talking about.

So it was my turn to zip-zip-zip, but with all of these unwieldy items of different sizes, shapes, and weights.

Luckily, it took our Nice Young Man a little longer to find a place than we'd all thought it might. With the shed constructed, he helped me move the bulky and heavy items from the tent garage into the new storage edifice during the next sunny weekend. Since my wife thought ahead, we had a bunch of metal shelving units that could either be transported whole or reconstructed in the new shed. With shelves lining the walls and room to store some items upright, I moved many things by myself and made room for others. I was able to store the leftover construction trash in the old tent shed and make room for more to go inside.

Would you like potatoes with your pot roast?

The party fridge broke in the summer of 2020, and sat looking dejected and horrible in our laundry room. On another weekend, the Nice Young Man helped me move it outside onto the deck. And move the shelf unit that had inhabited the living room since this time last year into its place. Eventually, we'll get rid of the refrigerator, but for now it sits on the back deck.

I'm not sure if this makes me trailer trash or just expedient. I expect there's a bit of crossover there.

Time for tacos!

The Nice Young Man found a place and moved out just before Halloween, so that freed up the guest room again for a little bit of storage.

I did end up having to move some of the heavy items by myself, but managed it because I am BURLY when I have to be. Also, I am strategic and was able to move the large items a little at a time or by deconstructing them when I could.

Also, I was unwilling to wait for the Nice Young Man to come to the house. And it feels weird and impolite to ask him to drive twenty minutes for dinner and then, "Oh! Would you move these things?"

With the living room settled so that we can now have a conversation and read a book (WHAT THE WHAT?!), I'm ready for my next leap.

The office needs my reorganizing magic.

I wonder if my Nice Young Man would like to join us for Thanksgiving.

"Weird and impolite" don't apply if you feed them AND let them watch football on the big screen.

·♥·♥·♥·♥·♥·

DRAGGY, FIGGY, FIGGY, DRAGGY

With the first killing frost on the horizon, I moved Figgy, our magnificent fig tree in a pot, from her sunny and prominent spot on the deck back into the dining room. While my strength doesn't always allow for such feats, her pot had lost a bit of dirt over the summer so I was able to drag her in all by myself.

But maybe I shouldn't start there.

After I shared my last piece about Figgy, a couple of things happened.

One morning, I opened the door for the cat and Figgy slapped me in the face. Her limbs drooped into the doorway innocently. Little happy fig leaves burst out across her spindly branches. Seeing these signs of good health, I did a thing.

I pruned her back.

Each of the drooping limbs that conspired in my slap were cut back to a promising leaf, most within a couple of feet from the dirt. The strongest branch I left standing, extended almost seven feet into the cool sunshine.

By pruning in the late summer, I knew I'd removed any chance of fruit for the year, but I wasn't expecting any, so no big loss.

When I'd finished, she waved her leaves and murmured, "Thank you for helping me get rid of that dead weight."

And she hasn't slapped me since.

One of you wonderful readers wrote and asked me the name of Figgy's gnome protector. This fine gentleman sits in the center of those now shortened branches, proudly guarding his domain.

Confession time! No idea what the little dude's name was! Since the original owners named the fig "Figgy," I assumed this small guy must be named "Gnomy."

But as soon as the words typed their way onto the screen, I heard a yowling "NOOOOOOOO!" from the direction of the pot. My fingers stopped their progress, and I vaulted out to the deck to confront the miniature fellow.

"Well." My body cast a shadow across his smiling face. "What is your name, then?"

With his most powerful voice (which was still a little squeaky), he proclaimed, "My name is Mondragon, the all-powerful. You would do well to remember that. You know what happened to the ones who came before."

Well, yes, I do know what happened to them. They moved to Connecticut, bought a nice little plot of land, and have a lovely life going with a garden and flock of chickens, ducks, and a turkey.

So Mondragon's his name. I call him "Draggy" for short.

Speaking of the former owners, they got back in contact after the last update and let me know a Very Important Fact. Did you know that fig trees smell slightly of cat pee NATURALLY?! All of that work spraying with the deodorizer! All of the blame on those interloping kitties! Oh! And now I have maligned those cats. However, they are gone so they will never know.

Unless one of you tells them.

Hey you!

Yes, I mean YOU!

Keep your pie hole shut!

Writing this piece reminded me of my plan to leave Figgy near the door so that, when people came to visit, I could say, "Oh no! That's not the cat's litter box. That's the fig tree!"

Or maybe I would just drop the fact casually. "Did you know that fig trees smell like cat pee?"

Well, with her in the dining room, I'll definitely mention it when people come to dinner.

Poor Figgy. Blamed for everything!

Over the end of the summer and beginning of fall, more and more little leaves unfurled from her branches, and when I moved her inside, her vigorous growth seemed unstoppable. She even managed to set a few tiny figs, which I'm sure she'll abandon along with her leaves in the shock of the transport. For now, with the one long strong branch lifting away from the rest, she looks like a very skinny lady with a full skirt and crazy big hat on.

Leaves never spread up that long branch, and when my mother-in-law visited, she recommended cutting that tall limb away. For the long winter inside, away from the majority of sunshine, I plan to follow her instructions. That course should allow for the tree to grow up and out a little without getting too leggy. Especially since she's back in the dining room.

There's just nowhere else in the house that she fits.

Though maybe she could sit in our newly organized living room. I wonder how she feels about being next to a couch.

"Hey, Draggy! Time to move again!"

Wait a minute. If he's so all-powerful, why doesn't he ever help?

·♥·♥·♥·♥·♥·

MOLLY THE SPIDER

Molly the Spider protects my yarn.

She moved into my office/craft room sometime back in the beginning of the summer. At least, that's when I noticed her web. This messy bit of elegance suspends itself between two shelves over my sewing kit. The web started under the overhang of a utility shelf. Molly wove her initial lair there, in the dark where I wouldn't notice.

In a bold move one night, Molly continued the web to a nine-cubby shelf that sits just about a foot away. The nearest cubby holds skeins and skeins of wool sock yarn. She ignores the other shelves with their knitting needle, book, and bead stashes. The web hangs toward the wall where bugs sneak outside of my notice.

Her web springs into the light with the dawn, a crazy orbit of strands looking more like a cobweb than the usual exquisite spiral. Later, in the artificial light of the overhead fixture, the web disappears into a shadow. Occasionally, I'll see her climbing upside down on the strong fibers, but mostly she remains behind the small overhang of the metal shelf unit.

I should probably inspect for a sack of babies, but for now I'm just letting her live her best spider life. I'm guessing she's saved my yarn by eating moth after moth.

But wait, a whole army of spiders protecting my yarn?

OMG. No.

Don't worry. I saw that as soon as I typed the words.

I'll do a quick search for that egg sac today.

Or maybe the spider is male. I always think of spiders as female, but isn't that just narrow-minded of me? A thought stuck in my head from *Charlotte's Web* as a child? Or is it biological? Do only female spiders build webs? Or only males? I probably should do some research, but opening Google seems like too much of a hassle.

In our home, we welcome most spiders.

Our spiders sit as sentinels in the (sometimes) dark corners of our abode. They feast on ants that come marching in through a crack hidden by the recycling bin, along the edge of the windowsill over the kitchen sink, and somewhere under the cabinets that allows access into the dishwasher. Their bellies grow full enough that they forget about some of the little ants strapped into their webs, leaving specks of carnage behind.

Our occasional cleaning lady knows that we welcome spiders and avoids their webs as much as possible. Before she visits, we always warn the spiders and let any who might have their webs destroyed know, so they can relocate. When she accidentally sucks a spider into the vacuum or rescues one by transporting it outside on her duster, she confesses immediately, filled with regret. "We warned them," we'll assure her. "They'll rebuild in no time!"

As she cleans the less-used spaces of the house, she chats with them, "Okay, spiders! Stay back. I like you, but I don't want to see you. And it's time to clean!"

I feel the same way.

Not the cleaning part.

While I appreciate spiders, I don't want to see them. I don't want them jumping out at me or crawling on me or any of that nonsense. Finding a spider touching me gives me the jumping creepy-crawlies.

Yes, it WOULD be funny for you. Just not for me.

You know how the ubiquitous "they" say that we eat however many spiders a night?

Again, not looking it up because LAZY, and also, I don't want to know that!

I want to think of myself as happily lying there, drooling around my mouthguard onto my pillow. If I thought about spiders moving in–or worse yet, dying!!!--in my mouth every time I fall asleep...

Ack! Ick! Bleah-bleah-bleah!

I imagine the little spiders, tied up in a Jabba the Hutt-style skimmer as the evil henchmen drive them to the hellmouth of terror. One looks at the other and smiles a confident grin while the evil villain tells them of the horror that awaits them past the teeth.

Even though I believe that the villain is the one who ends up pushed to his doom by the cocky resistance fighter, it still feels yucky.

After all, I'm the one eating him.

Yuck.

In North Carolina, we do have a few poisonous spiders that haunt us. After meeting the black widow that time, I always don my thick leather gardening gloves to pull anything out from infrequently used storage areas.

The black widow suspended herself in the air above the sacks in the trash can, her red hourglass mark beaming in the sunlight.

I jumped back and the lid thumped closed.

Dammit. Time for my big girl panties.

I opened the lid of the trash can again and positioned it in the full sunlight of the driveway.

"You have to go. We can't have you around the pets, and I know you don't want to be seen with us."

She put her little spider legs on her hips. "Close the lid. I like the dark."

"The lid stays open. Find another place to live."

Until it was time for the trashman to show up, the can remained as it was. When the day came, I looked inside and she wasn't there. With a sigh of relief, I closed the lid and took the trash can to the side of the road for pickup.

After the truck had pulled through, I noticed the trash can on its side in the driveway, flung with the lid open. The trash was gone, but the spider remained. She sat on the edge of the can, shaking her legs in triumph at the fleeing utility worker.

Oh no. Not at my house.

I hefted the trash can upside down and thumped and hollered. Then the can stayed open overnight so the light of the sun could get in there for as long as possible.

She found another home at last.

And thus the line was drawn. No poisonous spiders allowed.

But the house spiders, with their small bulbous bodies and long legs, they can stay. Eat all the ants and moths and other small pests you can capture, ladies!

After all, a girl has to have some standards. Even if she is the hellmouth.

Time to call our housecleaner! We have guests coming. Can you clean the guest bathroom shower? There are at least a dozen spiders in there.

Leave the office be. Molly is enjoying a moth!

Relaxing in the Afterglow with Lazy Leftovers

My favorite part about Thanksgiving is the aftermath.

Don't get me wrong! Thanksgiving Day and its feast, connecting with family and friends, watching Macy's big parade and crying at the Broadway numbers and the marching bands—I rejoice in these traditions. Even the massive amount of work, planning out the week, waiting in the grocery store lines (watch out for elbows!), baking pies and rolls, finding space in the refrigerator for the turkey to brine, the day of chopping and cooking and serving and cleaning—my tired body smiles as I collapse at the end of the day, usually with a glass of wine or brandy accompanying my tea.

The work makes me feel like I deserve that rest, for the evening and the whole next day.

The Whole Next Day.

With the pressure off and the work done, all I have to do is enjoy the bounty and hit the "on" switch on the dishwasher.

Oh yeah. I love waking up the morning after the feast, rolling out of bed and making myself a cup of tea accompanied by a piece of pumpkin pie topped with the slightly sad leftover whipped cream.

Gotta eat your veggies!

Lunch could be a slice of turkey smeared with cranberry sauce on one of my homemade dinner rolls, with a side of leftover carrots from the crudité platter.

And dinner. Oh, at dinner, Le Beau Mélange! That turkey gets accompanied by all the remaining sides, smothered with gravy, and warmed in a pie plate going directly from the oven to my TV tray. The last glass of the gorgeous wine opened especially for the holiday slips past my lips as I watch another Christmas movie!

For several years, the day after Thanksgiving ended with a visit to the neighbors for "Lazy Leftovers." Our pile of leftovers combined with theirs to make another feast! Two different kinds of dressing? Pumpkin, apple, pecan, AND chocolate chess pie? Yes, please! My neighbor's wild rice stuffing was to die for, and everyone devoured skinny slices of the multiple pies I could never resist making.

After all, a skinny slice of pie has no calories, RIGHT? Let's all agree on that.

We'd wear our jammies and drink all the already opened wine bottles (maybe even cracking open a new one) and talk and giggle and rejoice in the bounty of our lives.

Just thinking of those evenings makes me cry so hard with missing them that my abdomen cramps.

Ouch!

What can I say? That wild rice stuffing....

This year, my mother-in-law (who has been a staunch Thanksgiving guest since we moved to North Carolina) was visiting my sister-in-law in California until the beginning of January. The Nice Young Man who lived with us for a few weeks this autumn visited his brother in Tennessee.

Thus, we were alone for Thanksgiving.

So I bought a fourteen-pound turkey.

Whoopsie-doodle!

Well, it's hard to find a smaller one. At least, that's my excuse.

Yep. I am fully prepared for my favorite time of year—Aprés Thanksgiving!

Once the day after has passed, I get a little more ambitious. My plans for the leftovers of this fantastic bird (which we dry-brined this year with yummy results) may include the following:

Tikka Masala - Grab a jar of this Indian sauce from the store. Chop up some leftover turkey and add in the rest of your roasted brussel sprouts, green beans (not in casserole), and any whole veggies you might have leftover. Sauté a bit of onion, drop in your leftovers, and pour the sauce over. Follow the directions to finish the cooking process and serve over regular or cauliflower rice. Yummy!

Turkey Enchilada Casserole - Make a mixture of chopped turkey, Monterey Jack cheese, cilantro, and green onion. Mix together one can each of red and green enchilada sauce. Pour a small bit onto the bottom of a greased casserole dish to cover the bottom. Put a layer of corn tortillas down and then half of the turkey mixture. Add another layer of tortillas and then drizzle sauce over. Add the second half of the turkey mixture. Then more tortillas, and pour the remainder of the sauce over the top. A thick layer of cheese covers the whole thing. Spray a piece of aluminum foil with cooking spray and cover the casserole. Put it in the oven at 375 degrees and bake for thirty minutes. Then, uncover the casserole and bake for thirty minutes longer, or until the cheese is completely melted and the sauce bubbles around the edges. Remove the casserole from the oven and let cool for five minutes to set slightly. Cut and serve.

Turkey Tacos - Sauté thinly sliced onion and red bell pepper in a skillet until soft. Add chopped turkey to the mixture and sprinkle with garlic salt, cumin, and chili powder to your preference. When the turkey is warmed through, spoon into warm tortillas and top with cheese and salsa.

Turkey Soup - After the meat has been cleared from the bones, cover the carcass and a chopped onion, carrot, and couple of celery stalks with water. Bring to a boil, top with a lid, and reduce the heat to simmer for an hour. Discard the solids. In a new pan, saute diced onion, carrot, and celery in a little olive oil (or turkey fat if you still have it) until soft. Deglaze the pan with a little white wine. Add the turkey broth and bring to a boil. At this point, we like to toss in those thick egg noodles found in the frozen section at the grocery store. When they are cooked, add chopped turkey and warm through. Slurp, slurp!

Oh, the annual Leftover-palooza!

Time to relax in the afterglow.

·❤·❤·❤·❤·❤·

THE DANGERS OF GAUGE

What is that floating past the window? Is it a silky scarf dancing through the air? A breath of frosty mist?

Wait! I recognize it now! That's my caution. I threw it to the wind last weekend when I cast on a new knitting project.

You see, sometimes I want to knit something new without worrying about making a gauge swatch or loading up my knitting equations or searching for stitch patterns. Just knit and be damned!

A "Save the Date" card arrived in the mail as Thanksgiving weekend drew near. A couple of lovely young ladies are getting married late next summer, and I began to ponder the knitting possibilities.

That's when Unravelisto, the Knitting Demon, seduced me.

I did TRY to resist. I put him off with a rummage through my stash. Maybe he would get distracted.

No dice! A little over 3500 yards of different tones of gray plus a silvery metallic tumbled out of the cubbies. Most of the yarn is a mix of wool and silk, and the metallic is wool and nylon. The yarns blend well, with a delicious softness. I expect a snuggly warm throw for watching a movie on the couch or tossing over shoulders to run out to the mailbox.

The yarn was selected.

Unravelisto winked at me.

Rascal!

A plain notebook sits on my coffee table for grocery lists, notable quotes, and moments of inspiration. I drew a couple of quick pictures and did a little research.

What kind of research? Thank you, social media, for letting me peer into the lives of these young ladies and study their backgrounds for clues.

Not stalking! Just curiosity to inform the creation of a piece that will suit them. Caring. That's what it is. Caring!

Despite Unravelisto's insistence that we didn't need to wait, math assisted with my design. A simple equation based on the amount of each color available determined the width of the slanted stripes.

The whole thing gets knitted diagonally, slipping an entire blanket through my needles from corner to corner. With enough yarn to produce a square suitable for a throw, I could relax and start...knitting.

No gauge swatch required!

I enthusiastically clicked away, knitting row after row of garter stitch (because fluffy and schmoozeley for snuggling). Unravelisto chuckled as the little triangle grew. He faded away in the bright moonlight, smiling at a job well done.

And that left an opening for the practical voice of Fiberiel, the Bright Angel of Knitting, saying...

A gauge swatch would be nice.

For those of you not in the knitting know, a gauge swatch is a little bit of knitting created to measure how many stitches and rows you will have in each inch, using your selected needle and yarn. A swatch that measures at least six inches square gives you an okay idea of how this particular knitted fabric will act. Elizabeth Zimmerman, the hallowed knitting guru, recommended knitting a hat as a gauge swatch for a sweater. You see, the bigger the better with a gauge swatch. And really, if you don't knit a gauge swatch, your entire piece becomes the gauge swatch.

That can be so disappointing.

I used to say "disastrous!" but that gives this knitting mistake a little too much power. Really, when you are knitting a sweater and it turns out not to fit you, it's just disappointing. It's not a disaster. You can give it to someone whom it does fit or unravel the whole thing and reclaim the yarn for another project.

Say, a throw for a young friend who is getting married.

Not that I'm using reclaimed yarn for this project.

Not that that would be a bad thing. After all, Lesbian Law #2: Reduce, Reuse, Recycle!

Anyway, back to the wedding afghan....

Since I know how much yarn I have, all I have to do is get to the halfway point on my supplies and then begin to decrease. Easy to the Peasy!

However....

Oh, Fiberiel! Stop with those "Howevers"!

HOWEVER, the other thing you do with that all-important gauge swatch is blocking. Blocking is when you wash the piece and lay it flat to dry. Usually, this means a soak in cool water with a gentle detergent that doesn't need to be rinsed out. After a kind squeeze to remove as much water as possible, the piece settles on towels (usually on my guest room bed) to dry naturally.

The blocking process helps to even out your knitting by allowing the fibers to bloom and the tension to ease. Different yarns react in different ways. Some barely change from the needle to the blocked end product. Others....

My sweater project bounces and accordions on the needle, but when blocked turns flowy and light. Each inch on the needles ends up somewhere around an inch and a half blocked.

This is why you knit up a gauge swatch—and block it—before you progress with your knitting.

Shut it, Fiberiel! I know what to do!

I'll block what I have of the piece after I finish the next stripe. That will give me the information necessary to complete the project in peace.

As I dunked that small corner of the afghan into the water, Fiberiel flexed her wings and flapped away to wherever Unravelisto was harassing another weak knitter.

A wisp of smoke filtered through the air and settled around my shoulders.

Oh! It's nice to have my caution back.

She's a snuggly and QUIET companion.

·♥·♥·♥·♥·♥·

UPCYCLING CHRISTMAS

This year, I'm planning a recycled Christmas.

Don't tell the capitalists!

While I absolutely love making or purchasing the perfect gift, this year, we're giving pieces found in our home.

Usually, our gift giving ends up being a scattered affair. My sweet wife orders gift cards for her sister and nieces because finding gifts that they'll like is harder than climbing El Capitan. I mean if you get to that summit, it's super awesome, but a misstep sends you falling with a bit of a sting when you hit bottom. And on the way down.

Besides, they LOVE to shop! It's two gifts in one!

Most everyone else welcomes my hand-knitted goods because they live places where snow falls sporadically. A hat or mittens or scarf always find a use, even by the children who toss them over their shoulders before making another dive into the gifting mayhem.

Except for that one spiky bright yellow hat I knit for my niece. I don't think that ever saw use. Maybe as a Halloween costume?

No wonder they flinch when I mention knitting something for them!

Now, you might think I'm just being cheap about the whole thing, but this idea is not about that. Well, it's a little about that, but also about realizing that we have SO MUCH STUFF and knowing that a lot of these pieces can find loving homes within our circle of family and friends.

With found gifts, a heart-centered archaeological dig happens inside your home. Re-gifting isn't about the object. These pieces sing to you of their chosen recipients.

Just like crafting! You know how a skein of yarn will reveal itself in a vision as a shawl, a pair of socks, a sweater? How your fingers itch to cast on that glorious piece every time you glance at it in your stash?

And even if you don't knit, remember that thrill when you finally discover the perfect gift for someone after searching for hours through shops?

That's it! But, you know, the shop is your house.

Consider this kind of gift-giving more akin to a mother bestowing that one special piece of family jewelry upon her child on their wedding day.

All of that is to say that the things we're selecting from our home to pass along to the people we love aren't just objects we don't want or need anymore. When the piece reveals itself, we know that it belongs to this other person. For whatever reason.

And if it happens to be something we neither want nor need, how wonderful is that?! One of the magnificent things about gift-giving is how giving a gift makes us feel good too. And if the pleasure is doubled because we cede ownership over that object we previously enjoyed? All the better!

This year, I'm using the holiday to pass along things that others will love and that I have hung onto for too long.

And my only expense is stopping by the Dollar Store to pick up gift boxes and wrapping paper! And shipping, of course.

Win-win!

Within our society, we're encouraged to see this sort of depleted-finances situation as a reason to make us feel drained and failed and ashamed that this was all we had to give.

Instead, I choose to see the gifts that fill our home. And I get to allow those gifts to find their perfect place. To leave our life and enrich someone else's.

So, it's a recycled Christmas for us. After all, Lesbian Law #2 is Reduce, Reuse, Recycle!

I think your niece would love this popover pan, my sweet!

·❤·❤·❤·❤·❤·

PATRIOTIC DOGSITTING

When you drive past my house, don't be surprised if you see an American flag hanging outside my door, the dancing sparks of fireworks, and a brass band playing a brisk Sousa march.

I am serving my country.

In late November, my wife saw a social media post from a gal who needed someone to watch her dog through December. Susan (not her real name) works for the U.S. Postal Service, sorting packages and cards for twelve-hour days until the holiday influx abates. Alone at home, her pup constantly paced, whined, and barked. Maybe it was separation anxiety? She needed a place for the dog to hang out with people all day.

Not to brag, but we're boring herberts who hang out at our house most of the time. And, if both of us are out of the house, most likely Mack the Dog is with us.

So when my sweetie asked me if she should get more information, I thought, "What's the harm?"

Susan offered us $100/week to take care of her husky.

That's grocery money. Tempting!

My darling messaged Susan and offered to make room for her pup over the holiday. However, someone else only five minutes from her home had offered as well. At that distance, she could visit the dog often. Relief spread across my body.

A husky is energetic and ready for play. I'd definitely be on the hook for longer walks, and walks any time she needed to "do her business." Whew! I could figure out groceries another way.

A couple of days later, my honey checked in with our hapless postal employee to make sure everything had gotten settled. *But it hadn't.*

Damn those good intentions!

Later that day, Susan introduced this gorgeous white and gray husky into our home. Freya dove into the house to explore as Susan assembled the large dog crate. With a regretful goodbye pet, she left.

Realizing this new dog remained behind, our Dolce Bella Kitty Girl took off for the guest room, pissed as hell! She barricaded herself underneath the bed there for a full day. In pity, I brought her food and water. For a little more protection, I blockaded the back section of the house with a couple of dining chairs.

With the security of an easy escape avenue, Dolce emerged, making her mrewerereer noise and hissing at the new dog. Freya backed right off.

Good girl!

Freya hadn't ever seen a cat before. The intrigue! The exoticism! The fascination! Dolce remains healthily wary, but she has little to fear from this rambunctious puppy.

Oh, did I mention? This good-natured husky is only a year old. With very little training.

During the first exploration after Susan left, Freya peed in the house. In twenty-four hours, I cleaned up after her three times, once right after we'd been outside to potty.

We have some training to do.

The first morning, I pulled out the lead so Freya could have some extended outside time (hoping to avoid more poop left in the house).

Luckily, I checked on her often so I realized she'd snapped her lead before she left the yard.

Thus starting a chase around the neighborhood.

I traipsed through people's yards and tried to coax her into my car with treats. Finally, a dog in a fenced yard attracted her attention. As she ran back and forth along the fence, I snagged her collar. Tossing the dog biscuit into the enclosure (Thanks for the distraction, you cute thing!), I popped her in the car and returned home, sweaty and tired and crying. What had we gotten me into?

I looked at my honey. "Am I not doing enough that you felt like you needed me to do this too?"

"We've done more for less," she responded.

Well, shit. That's true.

Resigned to the lack of a lead, I took the dog out to go potty again. And again. And again. And again during our weekly crossword puzzle time with Dad. We spent three days learning how to hold it, but I'm still on alert.

Now, time to burn off some of that energy!

In the past, I enjoyed hour-long morning hikes with my pups. Those sorts of jaunts would be perfect for Freya! But that was years ago.

These days, my little couch potato, Mack the Dog, joins me on a twenty to thirty-minute morning walk followed by his morning nap. Freya's energy means new, longer walks that are tiring us both out!

But Mack doesn't resent Freya. Nope, he even plays with her after a restorative snooze, leaping and jumping and trying to hump her. Each time I see him attempting this move, I think of how his Chihuahua father must have appeared when he made his move on the Blue Heeler mama. "That's a whole lot of woman! Yeehaw!"

But my lagging energy caused a moment of slipped concentration on our Monday morning walk, and Freya slipped out of her collar.

Off on another merry round of tag around the neighborhood!

I walked up and down hills, drove over streets I never visit, stalked her through other people's yards. Once glimpsed, she would run at me, whipping by so close that I could almost grab her.

Freya loves that game.

So I stopped playing. I stood still on the hillside at the bottom of our property and closed my eyes. She zipped by me, brushing my hand with her tail. Through a combination of my stillness and her fatigue, I managed to grab her by the scruff of her neck and get the collar back on. Freya panted happily as we returned to the house.

Time for the no-pull harness. A dog trainer introduced me to the no-pull harness three dogs ago, and the first time I felt Freya hit the end of her leash, I knew I was going to need one.

No-pull harnesses do a couple of things. First, they reduce the strain on my arms and allow me to have control over the dog. Second, they remove the point of pressure from the dog's esophagus (which can cause injury) and put it under their legs. Each pull from the dog causes the straps on the harness to pull up under their leg pits (is that what they're called?), kind of like someone grabbing you from behind underneath your armpits. Uncomfortable, but not painful. And pretty much incapacitating.

Now we're walking instead of dragging Auntie LA down the street.

Another small victory!

And the small victories are building on each other. While Freya remains intrigued by Dolce, she's learned "Leave it" and is mostly leaving the cat alone. We haven't had an "accident" in three full days. And, last night, we fell asleep in a pile of people, dogs, and cat.

Meanwhile, I know that Susan is at the post office, sorting packages and cards to get them to all of us in time for Christmas.

I am serving my country.

Is there a medal for dogsitting?

· ❤ · ❤ · ❤ · ❤ · ❤ ·

HAPPY MERRY MOVIES!

D id you know that the first day of Christmas is actually Christmas Day?

I discovered this fact as a young adult. Listening to the folks over at NPR do their annual "gifts for all twelve days of Christmas" story, my mind began churning with the question. What are the twelve days of Christmas? When do they begin? When do they end? Are they continuous or do they show up one at a time throughout December and maybe January?

Much later in life, I connected the facts from my religious childhood. That the Christian season of Advent led into Christmastide which starts on Christmas Day. From December 25th through New Year's Day and into January, a raucous party roared celebration with feasts, gift giving, parades, and even trick-or-treating! The season ends on January 6th, aka Twelfth Night.

Which is Shakespeare's attempt at writing a Hallmark Christmas Movie.

Or so say scholars....

All of this is to say that, if you wish, valid reasons exist to enjoy the Christmas season all the way to January 6th.

With that in mind, I'm sharing a few of my favorite Christmas movies for your enjoyment. I seek these movies out each year and mumble the words to myself as the characters say them on the screen. Lately, my wife's conversations have started incorporating the same quotes.

"We had a case of carnations last week that ended badly."

"Catastroph!"

"It's pronounced 'Tay-Ah-Tee-May.'"

The Shop Around the Corner, 1940

This lively, comic love story centers around a man and a woman who work together, clashing at the shop while, in their private lives, they fall in love through a series of anonymous letters. In different eras, entertainment moguls remade the film as *In the Good Old Summertime* (perhaps the worst-named movie of all time), *She Loves Me* (a Broadway musical that is So. Much. Fun! But titled so that it doesn't quite explain anything), and *You've Got Mail* (which is the only title that actually manages do what a title is supposed to do).

The reason I love the original is because the darkness lives so close to the light. The secondary storyline is about the shop owner, who suspects his wife of having an affair. His decision to attempt suicide (I'd tell you why but SPOILERS!) makes the joyous conclusion so much sweeter, a great reminder of how precious we humans are to each other. This lovely movie stars Jimmy Stewart and Margaret Sullavan, and the entire ensemble's superb acting can almost make you forget the film is in black and white.

FYI—Everyone survives and I promise you will giggle.

Christmas In Connecticut, 1945

My absolute favorite Christmas movie of all time! Barbara Stanwyck stars in this comic story of a writer purporting to be a wife and mother who pens a wildly popular cooking column for a woman's magazine. However, she's no wife, mother, or cook! She's a career woman living in an apartment in the middle of New York City. The recipes come from her "Uncle" Felix, a restaurant owner (played by S.Z. Sakal). When the publisher of the magazine, a forceful magnate played by Sydney Greenstreet, sends her a sailor to entertain for Christmas, hijinks ensue!

This one tops my charts because the main character is a strong and independent woman writer willing to do anything to save her career. Even at the inevitable happy ending, I never believe she'll be anything but a writer. After all, as Uncle Felix says, "She can't cook, but what a wife!" Plus, the whole thing ends with Sydney Greenstreet chuckling like Santa and saying, "What a Christmas!"

The Hogfather, 2006

Based on the novel penned by Terry Pratchett, this satire of the Christmas season zings through an adventure where an assassin (Mr. Teatime, see above for pronunciation instructions) contracts to kill the Hogfather (aka Father Christmas in our dimension). Oh! Wait! To fully understand, you need to know that this whole thing takes place in Pratchett's Discworld in a city called Ankh-Morpork.

To maintain the balance, Death (voiced by Ian Richardson) takes the Hogfather's place, riding around the world in a flying sled pulled by boars. Michelle Dockery plays Death's Granddaughter, who is desperately trying to have a "normal" Hogswatch night as the nanny for two precocious children. A funny, deeply felt, and thought-provoking film that entertains multiple generations, as long as they appreciate fantasy.

And, now that we've been watching it for several years, our usual after-dinner tea and dessert gets called "Tay-Ah-Tee-May."

***

As you traverse that dreamlike time between Christmas and New Years Day, I give you these three recommendations to discover and enjoy.

Happy-Merry, my friends!

·♥·♥·♥·♥·♥·

CLEANING UP FOR THE NEW YEAR

O ur refrigerator was a pit of despair.

The depth and breadth of this larger-than-average fridge means that we can spread out all of our immediate food in a thin layer at the front of the shelves. However, anything that falls to the back is lost. Jars and containers with questionable and disgusting contents lined the back wall. Mysterious stickiness coated areas of shelves, and a dark brown goo outlined the bottom shelf where leaking substances had seeped under the glass.

Something had to be done.

And I was the only one to do it.

Icky. And something I could forget as long as I kept the refrigerator door shut. Or just looked at the front of the shelves.

Maybe we could just buy a new one?

But then, I got inspired.

Watching a television show, I was reminded of the tradition of cleaning the house before the New Year. The idea of leaving the dust of last year in last year and beginning the new year with a clean home seduced me. After all, I could use a little clutter clearing.

And those disgusting fridge shelves worsened each day.

For this final week of the year, I decided to take whatever energy I could muster and do a little deep cleaning—including the refrigerator shelves. My resolution wasn't to start something at the new year, but rather to do a little cleaning before that new year arrived. And in that process to clean at least one refrigerator shelf each day.

That seemed doable. Five shelves. Five days.

In the post-Christmas/pre-New Year's dreamtime, with the dog we were babysitting gone, my body relaxed and slept for hours. I woke late, meeting the day with my sweetie and enjoying a leisurely brunch.

Therefore, it was almost a surprise when I found myself circling our "kitchen island" on Monday, plotting and planning to deep-clean and reorganize that area.

I have to put quote marks around the label of "kitchen island" because I don't think anyone else in the world would call it that. To construct it, we pushed a metal prep table against a heavy-duty construction shelf. Providing ample storage and handy workspace, these two pieces anchor our kitchen area and allow us to chat and watch television together (as the kitchen and the den are actually just one large space). But if you don't look too closely, the combo blends with the stainless steel appliances to give the feel of an authentic restaurant kitchen.

Actually, with the construction shelf and wire rack storage, it might mimic an authentic restaurant kitchen a little too closely.

Brad Pitt entertained me from the den (*Moneyball,* 2011—good but not earth-shattering) while I rearranged and tossed and swept and mopped. When the entire "island" gleamed with cleanliness, I put it back together. With other pieces channeled into their correct slots around our property (interior design code for "I put a bunch of shit in the shed"), the stock pots and cookie cutters were able to nestle in under the prep table.

The newly reorganized and cleaned "kitchen island" didn't look much different unless you knew it well. With the majority of the work having taken place below the surface, even my darling didn't notice (though she was still effusive with her praise) until she was able to wheel by the prep table without getting snagged by the cardboard boxes that used to live underneath.

Riding on the upward swell of energy from this triumph, I cleared off a shelf of the fridge and scrubbed it clean.

One down!

And then I collapsed for the rest of the day.

Still in recovery, I didn't start my next cleaning project until Tuesday afternoon. Our cluttered entryway needed attention. The pile of random stuff gave way as I created new slots for the things we wanted to keep. Gardening tools to the shed. A beautiful old cachepot for a "hey, that's on sale!" lemon tree still needed to be filled with the lemon tree, but could move into the living room for now. Rechargeable batteries to the laundry room for storage in the house. Old house and bathroom rugs to the linen closet.

Everything moveable got moved, everything trashable got trashed, and a sweeping and mopping ensued. Once everything went back into its place, the space didn't look that much different, but it felt clean and bright and new and shiny. Each time I pass through it, I smile at the change and feel happy.

Which is what happens when you are an adult. Lord, I still can't believe that I've come to this place. The same feeling of pleasure and achievement I remember filling me as a child when I won a blue ribbon, that feeling is what hits me when I look at that cleaned-up and organized area of our home.

In the after-dinner haze of dishwashing, I cleared and scrubbed another shelf from the fridge. Two done!

After the two days of triumph, Wednesday delivered an almost full day of relaxation. A quick outing resulted in new groceries, so I cleared and cleaned the middle shelves (two half-shelves that equaled one full shelf) before storing everything away.

Two more cleaned! The only one that remained was the bottom shelf with its brown ooze.

Thursday dawned with a new vigor. I even woke up at my regular time!

With an easy morning of pleasant work behind me (as I'd been do-ing little dribs and drabs of actual paid work throughout the week—a self-employed person is never without something to do!), I confronted the bottom shelf of the refrigerator.

At least two jars tore away from the shelf with a ripping squawk of grossness, leaving half-moons of sticky, solid something behind. When I attempted to lift the glass from the shelf, it held firm. Worse yet, the shelf unit attached to the inside wall! What could I do? I filled a bucket with hot soapy water and began to soak and scrub.

A half-hour later, the surfaces that I could access were clean and sparkling but the gross brown lines remained. My honey came over to inspect the results.

When she reached underneath and pushed, I held my breath. A great cracking rang out and I closed my eyes.

"There we go! You see! You just needed a bit more strength. And I'm sure the warm water seeped down and made it possible." My astounding love stood triumphant, holding the glass part of the shelf up for me to see.

She'd done it! And the glass hadn't broken!

"You're a miracle!"

Thrilled, I pushed her aside and pulled the glass from the refrig-erator. Careful washing of the glass and the rest of the inside surfaces followed. A little lip holds the glass in the plastic frame of the shelf, and

I held my breath as I forced it into place. But I prevailed! Triumphant, I left the shelf bare for a few hours and gasped at the sparse beauty each time I opened the doors.

To calm myself after the excitement, I pulled out the vacuum and sucked the dust out of the rest of the house.

And that did it. My exhausted body collapsed onto the couch.

While the house isn't as tidy as I'd hoped for, at least I finished the refrigerator.

The rest can wait until next year.

·♥·♥·♥·♥·♥·

THE 4AM BOOK CLUB

One effect of my wife's stroke is that she wants to go to bed earlier, and these days, I don't mind. When I was working outside of the house, I felt like I woke up, left the house, came home, ate dinner, and then BOOM! Bedtime again. It seemed like sleep was the only thing I did in our house, except for on the weekends. But working from home, early bedtime feels less like a burden and more like the life of an old bohemian. After all, doesn't it feel a bit radical to go to bed early?

How early?

"Early bird special" early.

"Any news happening after 8pm can wait until the morning" early.

"How does my eighty-two-year-old mother-in-law stay up later than me?!" early.

Most evenings, we watch television and I knit until around 8pm. Then, this happens:

Me: Should we go to bed and watch TV for a while in there?

Wife: Well, it is more comfortable for me to lie down after sitting in this chair in the den all day.

Me: Let's go.

A few minutes of closing down the household and then we toddle off to the bedroom. We may watch another hour of television, but I'll be asleep before ten.

Most times before nine-thirty.

Okay, nine.

That's another thing that happened! Once the blankets cover me, my body relaxes and my eyes begin to close. Sure, I watch TV for a while, but sooner rather than later I am battling my eyelids and boom, I'm asleep.

But then I wake up at two or three in the morning and can't get back to sleep for an hour or two. Or don't get back to sleep at all. And I'm not worried or sad or anxious. I'm just naturally awake.

Recently, I read *Harlem Shuffle* by Colson Whitehead. In that book, the main character talks about a time he called the "Dorvay" and then cites a French word, *dorveille*. He uses this word to refer to the time between sleeps, also called segmented or broken sleep.

Before electric lights made the night a friendlier place, folks would go to sleep not long after sunset and begin their daily work just after dawn. In the long nights of deep winter, this could mean many, many hours in bed. During that time, most people would wake up for a couple of hours and do quiet activities until they fell asleep again.

This magical Dorvay time has intrigued me ever since I discovered it was a thing people once accepted as a normal part of life. My research helped me discover that, according to sleep researchers, our bodies naturally fall into this segmented sleep.

The idea of waking and then writing, reading, praying, meditating, doing hand-work, even visiting with their neighbors! In some places, lit candles in windows indicated that those inside were open to visitors during that waking time.

So I like to think I've joined my ancestors in the "waking up in the middle of the night for a couple of hours" tradition. While many of the historical figures who followed this practice used this time to write books, make discoveries, or engage in other brilliant activities, I read novels and memoirs.

Yep. I'm a real go-getter!

Part of me wants to keep my brain in that dreamy state where it's possible I might fall asleep again. I also like to think I'm tricking my body into believing that I stayed asleep and got all of the rest I needed, with novels becoming dreams that are just written by someone else.

Whatever the actual case, I finish books during this time. Because the light from my lamp might disturb Stephanie while she's sleeping, I read on my tablet or phone. Luckily, the ephemeral bookshelves on my cell contain so many books. Combine those connected with bookshops with access to my local library's electronic editions, and my early morning hours fill with more words than anyone could read in a lifetime.

Of course, not all books are suitable for that time or day or state of mind. In those dreamy pre-sunrise moments, I try to find reads that lull me back to sleep. Something I can read for an hour before nodding back off. Nothing too strenuous.

Scary novels don't work for me during that time. Especially great ghost story writers like Simone St. James. I tried to read *The Sun Down Motel* during this magical time and I ended up scared senseless, stuffed under the covers and trembling. Those are daytime, full-sun-out books.

The ones that work the best for me may be a little challenging. After all, I read the Colson Whitehead book during that time. But mostly I want a predictable outcome. The bad guys will lose. The good guys will win. The murderer will be caught. The memoirist will overcome the horror. The fantasy adventure will end with a triumphant yawp heard across the universe.

(Full disclosure: I read the last page of *Harlem Shuffle* first to make sure the protagonist got some kind of a pleasant ending.)

My favorites during this time slip into a lyrical space. Their stories and writing hold a positive, uplifting quality. For example, this morning I finished Becky Chambers' novella, *A Psalm for the Wild-Built*. Her books dunk me into a science fiction world where I'd love to live, surrounded by aliens and artificially intelligent beings who all have their own issues and workings. Hers would be literary fiction if they didn't take place in a whole other universe. Or rather, the universe of the future? Maybe? Her stories are warm, inviting, inclusive, and philosophical.

But between every Becky Chambers and Colson Whitehead, there's a cozy mystery, YA fantasy, detective story (usually about a woman during or between WWI and WWII who was a spy for the Brits. Not that I have a specific type). Though, within those genres, I search out books written by people with different outlooks than me, specifically people of color, people from other cultures and times in history, and people in the LGBTQ+ community (which I am a part of, but feel estranged from most of the time). These same books usually celebrate those other cultures and traditions, and teach me so much!

Learn while you sleep, right?! It's everyone's dream!

Since sometimes I go back to sleep for that second shift and sometimes I don't, I'm not sure if I qualify as a person practicing segmented sleep. But the thought alone that this is actually a really normal thing, a natural phenomenon, makes me feel better about getting up and going about my day.

In the last article I read, someone called it "getting two mornings."

Oh! How that thought delights my productive little soul!

· ❤ · ❤ · ❤ · ❤ · ❤ ·

HOW AN OLYMPIAN MADE ME WALK 500 MILES

I n 2013, I hiked 500 miles. Sure, some of those hikes were more walks than hikes, but every mile counted that year. My dogs, Cappy and Ty, traveled with me, and probably doubled my mileage as they ran back and forth along the trail. Gotta check on Mama when we're in the wilderness! There are bears and moose and elk in these woods!

During that year, I walked streets in towns and cities. I strolled along the Continental Divide and climbed a set of forgotten steps in the middle of Asheville, North Carolina. My father and nephew hiked with me to peaks in Colorado and West Virginia and along a portion of the Appalachian Trail.

Despite getting started after Easter, the dogs and I hit our 500-mile goal on a snowy day the week before Thanksgiving, at the entrance of an abandoned uranium mine outside of Steamboat Springs, Colorado. A friend accompanied me on that hike, and our smiling faces shone all the way home.

But it never would have started without the random gaze of an Olympian.

Steamboat Springs is known for its Winter Olympians. As far as I can tell, the geography and the environment combine in an alchemy that shoots them, fully formed, out of the local hot springs.

People tell me this isn't actually how it happens but, in any event, the area produces many athletes best suited to the Nordic skiing events. Those are the ones where the athletes fling themselves down long snowy slides to fly through the air and then race across the plains on skinny, long skis, waddling like panicked ducks as they travel uphill.

If I wasn't careful in Steamboat, conversations suddenly turned into deep discussions about which wax worked the best and why the ramstamblers on their Turbo Whackers helped them skate-ski faster.

Or maybe that's just what it sounded like to me? Rather than pretend to engage, I would attempt the classic Ninja Introvert, backing away and fading into the background until the conversation circle closed in front of me and I could flee.

But if I made an error, people noticed me and asked if I'd ever gone cross-country skiing. Which led to an embarrassed "No." My defense? Oh, I've always been interested in snowshoeing but darn, no snowshoes!

Because they never, ever believe that I moved to a place where feet of snow fall every winter simply because snow is pretty to gaze upon out my window as I sit in my warm comfy chair, reading and knitting and sipping hot tea.

And that's how snowshoes showed up like magic at my house one day.

They sat unused until 2007, when a precocious border collie/Australian shepherd mix puppy named Cappy wiggled his way into our lives. We needed a little doggy energy. What I didn't know was that I'd signed up for a LOT of doggy energy. Upon waking each morning, his eyes met mine over the side of the mattress. Every single day. Rain or shine or snow or sleet or below zero temperatures.

Time for our walk, his eyes would say. Let's go!

My out-of-shape body's saving grace was a frisbee. Each morning before work and each evening after, I took him out to the street and threw the frisbee down the hill. He leaped and twirled in the air to catch the flying disk. Standing in the middle of our quiet dead-end street allowed me to run him up and down the small hill our house sat on, and was the only way to get enough distance to tire him out.

To make myself feel less like a lump as I played with the dog, I began walking in place while Cappy ran after the frisbee. After a few weeks of this, jogging was possible. I'd bounce in the street, swooping down to snatch the soft disk from Cappy's mouth and flick it back into the air. Exercise! Yes!

At the bottom of our street, a house sat at the "T" with its front door facing up our hill. A young family lived there, and the father was Todd Lodwick, a Nordic skiing Olympian. In 2010, his Nordic Combined team won the silver medal at the Olympics.

So one day I'm playing frisbee with Cappy, using this little piece of plastic to save my fat ass from walking, and Todd Lodwick comes out and sits down on this bench outside the front door.

I notice him staring up the hill at Cappy doing his amazing catches and thrilling chases.

And all I can think is how silly I must look to this amazing athlete with my round little blobby body tossing the frisbee, jogging in place to exercise while my energy-filled dog spins to snatch the frisbee out of the air.

How could I not just walk the dog like a normal person when this dude watching us had tuned his frame into a serious athletic tool? How could I feel like WALKING THE DOG was too much for my body to bear when there, at the bottom of the hill, sat a person who pushed his body to the limit for the glory of hanging a little piece of metal around his neck?

How embarrassing for me!

The next morning, Cappy began getting walks around the neighborhood. First, we meandered around an area where I didn't have to climb hills. I slowly built up my strength so when I tramped down a steep hill, I could get back up it. We wandered down alleys to a small trail in the middle of town. Slowly but surely, we extended the length and difficulty of our hikes until I could make it up mountains to views where the town lay below me like a carpet and the peaks of the Rockies greeted me at eye level.

Ty, a small golden terrier, joined our family in 2009, and in 2013, the three of us hiked over 500 miles together.

But it never would have started if Todd Lodwick hadn't walked out onto his front porch and sat down to contemplate the view up the hill. He probably didn't even notice me, just Cappy leaping for the frisbee.

But that moment got me moving. And I will always thank him for that.

Even though I sat my ample booty down again afterward, and hiking those mountains feels like a distant dream.

Perhaps it's time for a standing desk. At least then I could walk in place.

And we all know where that could lead.

· ❤ · ❤ · ❤ · ❤ · ❤ ·

PSYCHIC JEOPARDY

D id you know that I'm psychic?

Let me demonstrate.

Each weeknight, Stephanie and I watch *Jeopardy*. At 7:30 here on the East Coast, we enjoy three contenders wrangling answers from their brains. Like the rest of the watching public, we guess the answers and rejoice when the correct response is so obvious to us but leaves the contestants clueless. At least once an episode, I scream random words like "Andrew Lloyd Webber!" and "Ararat! Mount Ararat!" at the screen, willing one of these people to hear me through space and time.

As you do. One of our friends posts his own yawps to the hapless *Jeopardy* contestants on social media every day, to the enduring entertainment of his friends.

My extrasensory powers unveil themselves when Final Jeopardy shows up. For Final Jeopardy, the topic of the clue is revealed and then the show breaks away for commercials.

This...Is...Psychic Jeopardy!

Oh yes! Psychic Jeopardy is my favorite part of the game (despite how I loooooove being a smarty-party and yelling the correct answer at the TV).

And you can play too!

To join us for Psychic Jeopardy, just guess what the final answer will be during the commercial break. For example, one day the topic was Twentieth Century Writers. Guesses could include Hemingway or Zora Neale Hurston or Judy Blume. All you do is sit with the topic in your mind for a moment and see what bubbles to the top of your brain. Bingo-Bongo! That's your selection.

Next, say it out loud so everyone in the room can hear.

If your selection matches the correct answer to the Final Jeopardy clue, you win Psychic Jeopardy!

Yahoo! Time for a victory wiggle and arm flail!

My father played Psychic Jeopardy with us for the first time during a recent visit. He got the answer right and amazed himself. "Well, shoot!" he exclaimed in his calm Daddy fashion. "See you in the morning." And, without any celebration, he headed back to the guest room to go to bed.

Oh, did I mention? *Jeopardy* is our last show before we retire to the boudoir. We rarely stay up past eight these days.

Remember when you were little and you were like, "When I grow up, I'm going to stay up all night long!"

And how whatever parent was putting you to bed would mumble under their breath?

That parent was laughing at you because they could barely keep their eyes open.

So, because we are normal adults with no other supervision, we move into the bedroom at 8pm to peruse a rerun of an old television show and drift off to sleep.

Right now we're working our way through the original *Mission: Impossible* series. Did you know that Martin Landau was considered a hottie? And Barbara Bain? Yes, please, I'd like some cinnamon on my toast. Rawr.

Since my little robin of a brain wakes me around 5am on most mornings (Stupid bird!), I am usually the one to pass out first. Depend on me snoring by nine.

My psychic prowess seems confined to *Jeopardy*. For example, sometimes in the few moments before *Jeopardy* begins, we'll view the last bit of *Wheel of Torture*—I mean, *Wheel of Fortune*. Despite the fact that I make fun of it for being easy, I am just shit at that game. I can never guess the word or phrase or any of it. But I wasn't ever very good at the Word Jumble either, so that makes sense.

Dammit, readers! I'm a humorist, not a cryptographer!

The other night, after I psychically deduced the answer to the final Jeopardy question (or is that the question to the final clue?), my wife jumped online and posted it.

Because, you know, it's impressive. Despite the fact that I didn't know if I'd gotten the answer correct until after Ken Jennings revealed it.

My sweetie knew. But she usually does.

Anyway, we occasionally post the feat to social media when Psychic Jeopardy goes our way. And then we discovered, we weren't alone! Soooooo many people got it right that night! And the first one to respond was a friend who proclaimed that she and her husband now play every night because I told her about Psychic Jeopardy.

Yep. I can see it now! People all over the world, laughing together and playing Psychic Jeopardy!

You know how I know?

I'm a psychic Lesbian Housewife.

·❤·❤·❤·❤·❤·

PARANOID OR REASONABLE?

With the mask mandate ending last week, I'm not sure how to proceed. Mask or no mask? If I wear my mask, am I paranoid or am I reasonable?

You see, my wife, light of my life, heart of my world, had a stroke back in 2017. That heart condition, piled on top of type 2 diabetes and a genetic lung disorder, makes her particularly vulnerable to COVID.

Score one for reasonable.

At the beginning of the pandemic, as soon as the first lockdown commenced, I skittered away from the office to work from home for the duration. And I never returned.

Actually, I lost that job because my bosses needed someone at the office and I was unwilling to come back while the disease still spun its way through the community.

And that's another one for reasonable.

FYI - No judgment either way on that front. They needed someone who could tolerate the risks of working in an office that was rarely public-facing, and I took the opportunity to spread my wings and fly like a penguin into the world of freelancing.

So you can see that I'm not entirely risk-averse.

Now that it seems like we're moving into a space where COVID is going to be considered endemic (meaning that we get to live with it around us like the common cold), I'm going to have to figure this out.

I don't mind my mask. It hides my chin hairs and silky mustache as they grow unabated while menopause takes its toll. Plus, I haven't had a cold in two years.

Let's give that one to reasonable.

But now that the state has ended the mask mandate, is the pandemic over? Can I go out without my mask? Is it time to invest in waxing? What's the deal?

I did some research on the CDC website. After all, I've gotten my three jabs, two for the initial vaccine and one booster dose, and so has my wife.

At the CDC site, I inserted my state and county and waited for the results. My county remained a high transmission area. Recommendations followed.

Wear your mask in public indoor settings. Wash your hands frequently. Continue social distancing. Get vaccinated as recommended. If you are experiencing symptoms, stay home and get tested.

When I went to the grocery store last weekend, people were in different states of mask wearing. Many wore them inside this crowded area, but others did not. And, as I walked through the store, unmasked people coughed and sneezed.

Okay. So that's NOT following CDC guidelines. But maybe they'd tested themselves and were negative for COVID? Maybe their outbursts were due to allergies or dust or the cold I've avoided?

I managed to calmly pluck broccoli from the produce section instead of following my first instinct, which was to leap out of the store like a superhero escaping an evil villain's ballistic missile.

Score one for paranoia.

After all, how many of us have coughed or sneezed at the grocery store? It happens. Why am I so jumpy?

Was it only a year ago that my vaccine safely protected me enough to chat unmasked at an outdoor business mixer and visit the grocery store with my full face exposed? Are those times coming back? Or does changing to an endemic approach mean they are gone for good for people like me who live with a vulnerable person?

For now, I'm going to continue as I have been. If I go into a crowded indoor space, like a shop, I'll wear my mask. Outdoors, I won't use it, just keep a bit of distance between myself and anyone else I meet. Handwashing will continue to be accompanied by the suave song stylings of me singing my A-B-Cs.

That seems reasonable, if a little unfair to the folks washing their hands around me.

So, if you see a little round lady flinching at your unmasked sneeze at the grocery store, know that she's simply attempting not to react like a mine exploded in the bread aisle.

Not to be paranoid about it.

·♥·♥·♥·♥·♥·

HAVE I MENTIONED THAT I DON'T LIKE CHEESE?

Yeah, it's not something that comes up regularly. Most people assume that cheese is a likeable thing. They eat it on toast and fruit and veggies and all sorts of stuff. Sometimes they even melt it down and just dip other food into it.

Sorry. I had to take a moment there. Ugh.

Now, I can handle a mild white cheese if it's melted or soft and has a strong flavor accompanying it. Brie covered with a sweet jam or nutty topping? Yeah, I'll eat that. Enchiladas with lots of sauce and savory fillings under the gooey layer of monterey jack? You betcha. An alfredo where the cheese flavor gives up under bacon or pumpkin? Yummo!

A cream cheese frosting has slowly gained my approval, but only with tons and tons of powdered sugar. The cheese must be the delicate tang that gives the frosting its complexity but doesn't overpower with the CHEESE flavor.

And during the pandemic, a quesadilla smothered with salsa became my go-to lunch.

I finally arrived in this "toleration/almost appreciation of cheese" space after fifty years of assault on this particular dislike. As a child, I wouldn't even touch cheese. The mere smell made me feel ill, and that clammy, soft-but-solid feeling creeped me out.

Pizza night was reserved for home, where my mother could leave the cheese off my part of the pizza. The tops of casseroles were peeled before going on my plate. Not enough cheese for everyone? No problem. Just don't put any cheese on my sandwich. Thank YOU!

As I grew older and more of my taste buds died, I began to be able to stomach a little cheese. Mozzarella melted on a pizza or meatball sandwich. A little melted Monterey Jack on top of a smothered burrito. But never just a hunk of cheese on a platter or cold cheese on any sandwich.

Just...ugh.

Recently, I went to a little café that everyone was talking up. Oh, it's so great! You'll love it! The food is so good.

I made my order for a chicken salad wrap. They did have a turkey sandwich with pear that might have worked, but there was brie. I mean, brie *is* one of the cheeses on my list and there were a lot of strong flavors around it which usually eliminates the cheese taste, but I didn't feel like it. When my plate came, the wrap was accompanied by a salad covered with feta.

Now, you might think that I can handle a little feta, and it's fine but not what I ever want, and did they have to dunk the salad in it? I brushed as much off to the side of the plate as possible.

Also, they grilled the chicken salad wrap. Who does this? And, no grapes or dried cranberries or anything to lighten the chicken salad.

I'm not a fan.

As my palate widened in other areas, cheese remained a sticking point. And the worst offender was blue cheese.

Once, my sister-in-law pulled a small wheel of soft blue cheese out of the refrigerator. "This is bad. We need to take it back." She held it up to display the black, mold-covered bottom.

In my defense, blue cheese always looks and smells like something that should be unwrapped and thrown directly into the trash.

"Is that how you tell? I haven't ever been able to tell if blue cheese has gone bad," I inquired with what I hoped sounded like innocence.

My sister-in-law detected the sarcasm. "It's black all across the bottom."

My penance for being a smartass decided, I returned the cheese the next time I went shopping.

Maybe I don't like blue cheese, but that's not the point. Everyone else seems to love it. My wife particularly likes it on top of pears as a dessert during the holidays.

I try not to look at her plate. Or sit near enough to smell it.

Last week, my mother-in-law came over with a snick-snacky lunch of leftover appetizers, a fresh salad, and a box of Trader Joe's fondue. It came in a cardboard box and slipped out of the metallic plastic bag with a slightly sucking blorp into the pan. I had to warm it up, and the smell reminded me of my childhood.

You see, when I was a kid, I loved horses. I was dedicated to horses. Each Christmas list to Santa included a horse. My parents decided to give me riding lessons when I was in elementary school, like second or third grade. Each Saturday, I would go riding and progressed in my abilities until I graduated from the slow mare to one of the bouncy ponies.

Anyway, one week I was so sick that my parents weren't going to let me go. I begged and pleaded until it was almost too late, and then my Dad came up with a brilliant idea. He told me that if I ate an egg salad sandwich (something I hated!), he would take me to my riding lesson. We were late, so he bundled me into the back seat of the car, and off we went. A few minutes into the ride, I handed him the bare plate and he was amazed! While riding horses, my body made a miraculous comeback, only to relapse on the trip home.

On Monday morning, after marinating for forty-eight hours in the Arkansan summer heat, the smell almost knocked Dad over when he opened the door of the car. I'd bamboozled him! He dug around and discovered the egg salad sandwich lodged under the driver's seat.

Yee-argh!

What I remember about this incident is that, even years after the car had been washed and dried and aired out many times, on trips when the windows had to be up and warmth rose in the car, the remains of the scent of that spoiled egg salad would drift into my nose.

That is the childhood sense memory the fondue unearthed.

Thanks, fondue. Thanks for the memory.

Even now when I consider the idea of enchiladas smothered in cheese to sound cozy and yummy, I still cannot even be near strongly flavored cheeses. The worst offenders are American, Velveeta (which...is it a cheese? Or a cheese-flavored product? I deny its ability to be food!), and blue cheese.

So, if you invite me over and see me digging into a particular selection of your cheese platter, you can feel proud.

That one probably doesn't even taste like cheese!

·❤· ·❤· ❤ ·❤· ❤·

WHY I LOVE FISTICUFFS

During emotional uproar, I find comfort in action-adventure entertainment. There's something about a show with tons of action but very little blood and gore that makes me feel better. I don't want reality. I want stories about star fleets, superheroes, and murderbots. I want cozy and cozy-adjacent murder mysteries, heist movies, and James Bond-style spies.

What do all of these have in common?

Fisticuffs.

I love me some fisticuffs! The guard getting knocked out with a karate chop to the back (WTF? How does that work, Impossible Mission Force?). That moment when the superhero gives the grand villain the final punch that sends him flying into a wall. A guy who surveys a crowd of tattooed muscle surrounding him and says, "Is this all you got?" before leaving the villians in a heap in the middle of a deserted warehouse.

Speaking of which, can we talk about Christian Kane? From *Leverage*? That heist show with the criminals who turned into do-gooders to get justice for people who've been wronged by big corporations or rich people with no care for their fellow humans?

Christian Kane plays Elliot, the Hitter. He's the one who leaves the goons in a pile.

This actor has since worked with Dean Devlin in several of his efforts including *The Librarians, Almost Paradise,* and *Leverage: Redemption.*

Recently, I was trying to figure out what the deal is with this guy. Why is he so attractive? Because he is an attractive man. And the reason that he's had so many jobs with this production company is because of his appeal to the ladies. They follow him on social media and ask about the next show he'll be in.

And suddenly, I realized what it is. In each of these shows, he acts and dresses like a lesbian.

Yep. Check it out. Even in the initial press stills for the first season of *Leverage,* his character wears a white button-down shirt and a VEST. A VEST, people!

As I watched reruns, I started seeing other signs. Cuff bracelets. Puka shell necklaces. Chunky watches. Cargo shorts. Plaid flannel shirts with t-shirts underneath and blue jeans. An affinity for horses and the women who love them. A tough who subdues his opponents and then empties the guns of their bullets, throwing them aside when finished.

One episode I watched even started with him nursing a bruise he'd received when he went to a lesbian bar. "How was I supposed to know it was a lesbian bar?" he protested.

The only surprising thing to me was that the lesbians hadn't welcomed him as one of their own.

And you can see this chic dykey fashion sense through all of the shows he's in under the Dean Devlin flagship.

As I did a little research, I found a message board discussing this actor and his sexual preferences. A little speculation that he might be gay. And this one person's assertion: "Well, unless you're him or part of his inner circle, you don't really know. He presents himself as straight, that is all I know. If he was gay or bisexual, I wouldn't really care. He would still be talented and supremely hot."

Which is, in fact, the right answer.

Because I know the secret...

Why do the ladies love Christian Kane?

The ladies love a lesbian.

No wonder I enjoy fisticuffs!

·♥·♥·♥·♥·♥·

ALERT FOR DEMOCRACY

I am an American, so why does the unexpected display of an American flag frighten me?

When I see someone driving around with an American flag on their car, a shiver zips through me. American flag pins on lapels warn me away from conversations.

And those t-shirts people wear with the flag drained of color or with weirdly toned stripes or angry eagles?

I barely resist the urge to run out of the grocery store screaming, "ZOMBIES!!!"

Instead, I take a deep breath and go back to checking the eggs for broken shells. You know, staying casual.

Because if you start screaming, they know you know.

Though, when I consider it now, the flag doesn't always scare me. A flag draped over the coffin of my uncle, a veteran of World War II, for example. His Admiral son arranged a twenty-one gun salute, after which that flag was folded in the classic triangle and handed to my aunt.

I watched with reverence. While my uncle hadn't died during his service, he'd cared enough to put his life on the line. He wasn't alone. All of his brothers served in the military. My grandparents sent two boys into the second world war, and one to Korea. Several of my cousins served in the military as well, and I feel deeply grateful to them for their service.

The knowledge that so many of my family members laid their own lives on the line for that flag fills me with pride.

During the pandemic, my country supported me and my health with mask mandates and stimulus payments that kept our little household going. During that same time, my state assisted me with a grant to pay my mortgage, my wife applied for Social Security, and we both received health insurance through Medicaid and the Affordable Care Act.

So, sometimes gratitude mingles with reverence and pride when I see the flag. It reminds me that this web of purple mountains and amber waves of grain is woven with lines of mutual support which, at their very best, touch every American. This flag isn't just for the red caps or lapel-pin wearers. These stars and stripes fly for ALL of us.

I am an American.

So I decided a few years ago to take my flag back.

The idea started when a friend gave me two pairs of wacky socks. She's been getting them for years, gifts from friends and children received with a sigh and a bit of a false smile. When she discovered my adoration of wacky socks, she began handing them over to me. I, of course, usually wear my own homemade socks, but these hand-me-downs are thin, perfect for the end of spring or beginning of fall. One pair of socks was blue with white stars and the other, red-and-white striped.

A little mixing up and voila! Now I have two identical pairs of patriotic socks! Blue with white stars on one foot and red and white stripes on the other.

"I'm taking my flag back!" I thought as I surveyed my outfit in the full-length mirror. All gray except for the socks, to make them stand out on election day, 2020.

Now, I have made fun of the people who wear flags as clothing. And nothing irritates me more than someone draped in the American flag with a bright red hat on, professing to be a "real American."

ZOMBIE!!!

Do you think I'm an alarmist? Because many folks I know whose relatives have embraced this authoritarian regime tell stories of how it seems like their parents or siblings or cousins aren't even there anymore. How they're just mouthing talking points they heard on Fox News. Accepting falsehoods as facts and disengaging from reality.

And, of course, you know the roots of the word "dictator," right? No? Oh, let's analyze the word for clues.

First there's the "dic," and here we must assume that the person who came up with the word simply left the "k" off because theirs was so small.

Have you ever noticed how dick can mean penis, but also dick can mean asshole?

The English language has a lot to answer for.

The second part is "tator," which we know from living in the South means "potato." Though they did get the spelling wrong—it should be "tater." I know this from a kid in my high school whose nickname was "Tater." He had a long-time girlfriend that folks occasionally called his "sweet tater," before going on to say that they would get married and have a bunch of "tater tots." She dumped him not long after I heard this joke for the first time.

I don't remember Tater's real name.

Anyway, these lie-embracing relatives have accepted the Penis-Potato as their ruler.

ZOMBIE!!!

Once I crossed that "wearing the flag" line for myself, those crazy flag socks inspired me to cast on my own sock design to express my hopes and fears for our country. Made from a sock yarn dyed by a small American business, the stripes are red, white, blue, pink, and a variegate of all of them.

To that mix, I added a fluorescent safety green for the heels and toes. Because we must stay on our toes to protect democracy! The forces of the Penis-Potato are constantly among us.

The socks sing of this ever-present danger. A song composed to elude the Zombie virus, to reach through the rhythms of authoritarian speeches and save those who can be saved.

The Penis-Potato wants our flag to frighten people. But I think of the fifty white stars on that flag. How every single state gets a star. How if a territory becomes a state (I see you, Puerto Rico!), we'll redesign the flag to add another star.

And I think of how those thirteen stripes stand for our history. The original states that banded together and fought for independence from a monarchy (a name for another sort of Penis-Potato).

This flag is mine, too. And I get to say that it stands for democracy. For inclusion. For a web of governmental service that supports all Americans and those who want to become Americans and those who visit, work, and learn in America. For a web of citizens who participate in this democracy by speaking up, serving as volunteers or employees or military or scientists or elected officials. By fixing what's going wrong. And by elevating and celebrating the good things like our national parks and the amazing diversity that exists in our culture and environments.

And those red hats following the Penis-Potato want to change that. They want to control what we say, who can say it, what we can do, and who we can do it with.

Stay alert for democracy, my friends.

Time to take back our flag!

I suggest starting with socks.

·♥·♥·♥·♥·♥·

ARE YOU WATCHING THE PAGEANTRY?

W hen I was a child, breaking news could ruin a Saturday morning. *Super Friends* or *The Smurfs* would suddenly be supplanted by a Very Serious News Face telling my parents about a Serious Tragedy or updating them on an Ongoing Important Situation.

Duh, News Face! My parents aren't watching *He-Man and the Masters of the Universe*. They are sleeping in.

They told us to turn the television down and don't wake them unless someone in our house is bleeding.

At eight years old, I remember one particular Saturday when the Papal Conclave gathered to elect a new pope.

WTF, Catholics? On a Saturday morning? Couldn't you at least wait until the afternoon?!

All my cartoons had been preempted by this coverage. While disappointed in this network decision, I remained riveted to the small black and white television. What color smoke would rise? When would they make a decision? Would it be before *Fat Albert*?

When they finally announced the election, I ran to my dad to tell him the news. He looked at my earnest little face and very kindly said, "That doesn't have anything to do with us. We're not Catholic, so it's all the same to me." Then he went back to reading his book.

Those words echoed in my mind this morning. The news that

Queen Elizabeth had died swept across my various screens. Even though I consider myself an Anglophile, being a fan of cinema, television, and books from the whole former British Empire, I feel sympathy for the nation but don't particularly grieve the loss.

Queen Elizabeth held herself to a stoic standard that kept regular folks at a distance in the best of times and was problematic in the worst. Many of us in the LGBTQ+ community found her reluctance to address issues central to our existence troubling, especially since her role was more symbolic than political.

At least she love-love-loved her corgis!

I watch the hubbub surrounding this moment and feel so sad for the family, as I wrestle with my own mother's death. To have the weight of an empire fall on your shoulders at the moment of loss must be a strange and horrible thing, even with years of preparation. And the shift in your own life echoes on the world stage with unknown consequences. After all, that monarchy has very little to do with the actual operation of the U.K. government.

Then again, I'm an American. We escaped British rule almost two hundred and fifty years ago, and we still celebrate that separation each year. Although Britain is now our closest ally, it is still another country and she was their monarch, not ours. While the pageantry is seductive and the coverage on both U.S. and U.K. news outlets pervasive, I'm not British, so it's all the same to me.

I guess my reaction is the reaction of a person whose friend's mother died. She was an amazing person, forceful and graceful, evolving with the times while integrating her social training from the past. I never felt very close to her, but she raised a fabulous country that I love, a being who created beautiful and fantastic art, who introduced me to my favorite secret agent, and whose grief in this moment is to be respected and shared in a very small way.

At the same time, this event reminded me of how our television lives have changed. Now, kids can watch their cartoons without having to wait for Saturday morning. Adults can tune into the news on whatever screen they wish.

In these days of apps and subscriptions, we choose what we watch with intention. We can tune in or walk away. It's up to us.

And yes, I probably will watch some of the funeral festivities.

I can watch my cartoons any time.

·♥·♥·♥·♥·♥·

THE NONBINARY RABBIT WARREN

A friend wrote to me and asked, "My son has explained 'nonbinary queer' to me several times, and while I understand it in
the moment, I'm confused again by the next time I see him. Can you
help?"

Oh, goodness. Yes, I can help, but I know your confusion is because
you've gotten caught in the Rabbit Warren.

*We use the term "rabbit hole" to indicate our curiosity
taking us on a trip into the bottomless unknown. We
could be following links to suggested shows on Netflix
or exploring the mysteries of bergamot or deciding what
pattern to knit next. All are rabbit holes. And all contain the possibility for confusion in their maze of corri-
dors and dead ends.*

*In conversations, rabbit holes can lead us into deep dis-
cussions of feelings, thoughts, and, if alcohol, caffeine, or
drugs are involved, weird logic circles that somehow end
up being prophetic. However, they can also lead us into*

states of confusion.

Definitions of social constructs often lead us down not just rabbit holes but the entire mazing burrows of rabbit warrens. The term that we needed defined leads us to other terms that need to be defined, and our questions pile on top of each other until we know the only way to clear them out is with a bonfire and WHY DID YOU MAKE THIS HAPPEN, STUPID WORLD? I ONLY WANTED TO UNDERSTAND!

We need to focus on one thing at a time. I'm going to define the terms *nonbinary* and *queer*. Sometimes you'll see a word you don't recognize. Don't let yourself get distracted! Read through these plain parts once without stopping, and then go back and read the whole thing, paying close attention to the italicized sections.

Let's get started!

QUEER

Queer generally means any person who identifies as something other than a cisgender, heterosexual person. The word is often used interchangeably with gay and LGBTQ+ (and all its variations), and had a pejorative use until the community reclaimed it.

The queer community includes a symphony full of variations on this theme, and nonbinary folks are part of that community.

It's like at a small church where there's a volunteer choir. A singer in the choir is a member of the church, but not all members of the church are in the choir. Queer is the church. Nonbinary sings in the choir.

The term "cisgender" means that your gender identification lines up with your assigned gender at birth. Its opposite is transgender. Cis is a Latin word that means "on the same side as." Trans comes from Latin as well, meaning "on the opposite side as."

Nonbinary people fall into the "trans" category, along with trans men and trans women, since their gender identity doesn't align with their assigned gender at birth. While we usually think of "trans" meaning transitioning gender, many nonbinary folks think of it as transcending gender.

Nonbinary

To truly get this concept, we've got to start with a biology lesson.

I know, right? Are we going to dissect frogs? Gross!

No worries. No dissection necessary!

Biologically, people can be born as male, female, or intersex. This is considered your biological sex. A person's biological sex can be different from their gender.

Intersex people are born with reproductive or sexual

anatomy that doesn't fit our typical definition of male or female. This can range from visibly confusing genitalia to mosaic genetics that might not ever be discovered. Yep, you could be intersex and not even know it. How about that?

Also PLEASE GOD NO, DON'T EVER SAY HERMAPHRODITE!!! This outdated term has been used pejoratively. The only people allowed to use this term are intersex folx reclaiming the word. (And no, reasoning that you could be intersex and not even know it so you can use that word doesn't count. Don't be an asshole.)

Gender is part of your social identity. While there is the binary of man and woman, many people understand their gender as encompassing both categories, neither, a fluctuation between the two, or even going beyond the binary categories entirely.

BOTH?! Yep. Nonbinary covers a range of people who may use terms such as *gender queer* and *gender fluid* to describe their gender. Gender fluid people typically don't have a fixed gender and may fluctuate between multiple gender identities and expressions. And sometimes they even let all of us in on which identity rules that day.

Gender expression is yet another level in the queer continuum. The way we express ourselves to the world might be masculine, feminine, or transcending the idea of gender altogether. Often, even if we have an idea of the look we're presenting, people who see us may make

*assumptions that gender our presentation. I mean, is
there anyone among us who hasn't tapped a man on the
shoulder at the hardware store and been surprised by a
butch lesbian turning around to help us in our quest?*

*People slide from masculine to feminine presentation
or combine these looks as they wish. To reject society's
presentations of gender altogether steals the breath from
my lungs. The sheer joy of Jonathan Van Ness (from*
Queer Eye) *as they swish across the ground with a perfectly coiffed beard and ankle-length skirt is as majestic
as the Grand Canyon and reminds me exactly why
some cultures revere these folks.*

*However, nonbinary doesn't require such a riotous pre-
sentation. These people dress in all sorts of different
ways, ranging from a more "binary" presentation to a
look like an older tomboy with androgynous outfits that
would fit right in at a lesbian bar in the 80's. LOVE
IT!!!*

A nonbinary person's gender typically falls outside of the
man/woman binary in some way.

*Frankly, most of us don't have a question about our
gender. In a recent Pew Research survey, only 1.6% of*

people (and 5% of young folks aged 18-29) were trans or nonbinary. However, a growing number of people know someone who is nonbinary, so visibility is rising. YAY!

Nonbinary people generally use "they/them/their" as their pronouns, though some use "she/they" or "he/they." If you are speaking to someone who uses "they/them" pronouns, where you might say "he" or "she," use the word "they." If you were going to say "him" or "her," say "them." If you are referring to something they own, use "their" rather than "his" or "her."

Wondering about someone's pronouns? Talk to them and ask them what they want to be called. We do this with everyone, actually. Not every Charlotte goes by Char. Some prefer Lottie and others prefer Charlie, thank you very much.

And what do you do when you use the wrong pronoun? It's just like when we were in France and I was trying to speak French to the local folks. I'd stumble through my halting phrases and end with an apology for everything I got wrong. The locals would kindly smile, correct my French, and encourage me to do better.

That's all anyone here is asking you to do. Nobody expects you to be perfect. Do your best to use the right

pronouns. When (not if!) you get it wrong, apologize,
correct yourself, and continue the conversation. If some-
one else corrects you about their pronouns, thank them
and do better next time. Don't make a big deal out of
it. Remember, it's not about you.

Nonbinary people can be sexually attracted to men, women, neither, or both.

Sexuality indicates who you are attracted to and how
that shows up. Sexuality is what we're talking about
when we say lesbian, gay, bisexual, asexual, and all
of the subsets thereof. Lesbians are women attracted to
women. Gay usually applies to men attracted to men.
Bisexual indicates people attracted to more than one
gender. Asexual means usually being sexually attracted
to no one.

That's the simple answer.

Of course, the not-simple answer includes this dive into
the rabbit warren of biological sex, gender, and sexual-
ity. And here I've only scratched the surface of the many
layers of the nonbinary and queer experience.

If you are here because you are wrestling with new
knowledge about a friend or relative, I encourage you to

find the joy in their revelation. This person is traveling a path many will not be called to tread. Just like all journeys, this one is filled with happiness and danger and fear and triumph. When they told you they were nonbinary, they invited you to be a part of their adventure. You can be an obstacle to overcome or a helping hand.

Choose to be an ally. Whether you are a jester or a knight or the housekeeper who greets them with their favorite oatmeal-cranberry-butterscotch cookies, your actions display your love and support.

It's that simple.

·♥·♥·♥·♥·♥·

EAT THE WHOLE COOKIE

I used to meet up with a client at a little coffee shop on the main street of Weaverville, North Carolina, a Mayberry-like town where we lived for seven years. The folks who ran the coffee shop would have made Barney's eyes bulge. Ladies with tattoos. Guys with ponytails and...a man-bun. However, if Barney stayed long enough to devour one of their delicious muffins, cookies, or chunks of chocolate chip banana bread, you'd find him there today, happily snarfing down a treat with his half-caf oatmilk chai latte.

Every order required running the gauntlet of baked goods lining the counter, so a treat accompanied every meeting.

After all, don't we deserve a reward for having to do business in the middle of the day at a pleasant place with someone we like?

One day, peanut butter cookies stood out among the phalanx of goodness. These cookies were the size of dinner plates, at least eight inches across with the correct mix of crisp outside and chewy inside. When my client arrived, he took one look at that generous bit of lusciousness and sprinted for the counter. "You can share mine," I offered as he grabbed one from the basket.

"Oh no! I have to have my own." He clutched the cookie to his chest.

Rewards aren't things to be shared.

When he returned to the table, he set down his cookie and grinned. "Eat the whole cookie," he stated. "Always eat the whole cookie."

With these words of encouragement, my delicious nibbling began. But, with this size of cookie, the delight becomes a slog about halfway through. When that happens, the other half gets re-wrapped in the plastic it came in and stored in my purse for later.

Because I will always eat the whole cookie.

When I was a child, my Aunt Leola used to make the most fabulous tiny chocolate chip cookies. Packed with chips and pecans, these little marvels measured about a tablespoon. They never melted down into a flat circle but remained mounded in a little pile, just as they landed on the cookie sheet.

At one point, my father asked for her secret (shortening instead of butter?), and he experimented. Eventually, he came up with a marvelous chocolate chip cookie, one good enough to attempt to launch a business with, but never managed to recreate the little heap of a cookie we both remember.

After the seventies, cookies grew. I remember being a teenager in the eighties and starting to see larger cookies on sale at counters in the mall. Pie-sized cookies appeared, meant to be decorated and used for birthdays and special occasions.

When my wife and I opened our internet café in 2001, the cookies we sold had to be at least five inches in diameter to be taken seriously.

Now, purchasing a cookie as a little treat has become difficult if not impossible. Most require the caloric investment of a regular lunch. I can't tell you the number of half-cookies I've found in my purse, wrapped in their leftover plastic or paper bag and crumbled out of recognition.

Of course I eat them. I'm a menopausal goblin who digs through her purse to find the latest cookie crumble when that midday sugar craving hits.

But I love a smaller cookie, one where you can eat the whole thing without feeling bloated. My cookies are small, by which I mean one to two ounces and with a diameter of about three inches. They resemble the cookies I remember from lunch boxes, cookie jars, and the platters at Sunday school as a child.

At this size, cookies are a delectable jewel instead of a slog. Their small size allows the flavors to collide on your tongue. For autumn, my favorite is packed with oatmeal, dried cranberries, butterscotch chips, pecans, cinnamon, cardamom, and nutmeg. They almost feel healthy until your tongue resonates with the sweet gem of a butterscotch chip.

With tea in the afternoon, one cookie perfectly fills your snack hole. You could even have one for dessert after lunch. And plan on at least two after dinner.

Eat the whole cookie. Just make sure it's a reasonable size.

·♥·♥·♥·♥·♥·

CRANBERRY BUTTERSCOTCH PECAN OATMEAL COOKIES

(MAKES AROUND TWO DOZEN COOKIES)

1/2 cup butter

   1/2 cup brown sugar

   1/4 cup white sugar

   1 egg

   1 tsp. vanilla

   3/4 cup flour

   1/2 tsp. baking soda

   1/2 tsp. cinnamon

   1/4 tsp. salt

   1/4 tsp. nutmeg

   1/4 tsp. cardamom

   1 1/2 cups oatmeal

   1/2 cup butterscotch chips

   1/2 cup dried cranberries

   1/2 cup chopped pecans

Preheat oven to 350 degrees. Cream butter and sugars together. Add egg and vanilla, beating well. In a separate bowl, combine flour, baking soda, salt, and spices. Add to the butter mixture and mix well.

Stir in oatmeal. Add chips, dried fruit, and nuts and mix thoroughly. Drop by rounded spoonfuls at least 1" apart onto ungreased cookie sheet. Press the tops of the cookie mounds to flatten slightly. Bake for 10-15 minutes until golden on the bottom. Allow the cookies to cool on the cookie sheet for one minute before removing them to a wire rack. Cool completely. Store in an airtight container.

These cookies can be frozen before baking. Put a piece of parchment paper on top of the cookie sheet and place them as above. Then place them in the freezer until the cookies are frozen through. Remove them from the cookie sheet, pop them in a plastic bag, and keep them frozen until you want them. At that point, put however many you'd like on an ungreased cookie sheet and bake as directed.

·♥·♥·♥·♥·♥·

ADVICE FOR COMING OUT DAY

I n my friend groups, I'm usually the Lesbian Friend. I don't mean for it to be this way. It's just how my life turned out.

Thus, I'm the authority on everything Queer (note the capital Q) for my straight friends. One by one during gatherings, people sidle up and whisper questions like:

"What's nonbinary queer?"

"Is Halloween the Gay Christmas?"

"Does every episode of *Glee* have to be so gay?"

First answer: See "The Nonbinary Rabbit Warren" on page xx.

Second answer: Every holiday is queer if you celebrate right.

Third answer: Yes.

Furthermore, as your Lesbian Friend, I feel obligated to inform you that October 11th is Coming Out Day.

Just in case you were wondering why your nephew decided to come out to you on a random Wednesday in October.

It's not random. It's National Coming Out Day!!

Back in 1988, a couple of LGBTQ+ activists, Robert Eichberg and Jean O'Leary, began National Coming Out Day as a positive expression of personal political action. After all, fear thrives in darkness and ignorance, and so did the AIDS epidemic. Back in the eighties, coming out of the closet and informing friends and family about your queerness put a face on that amorphous LGBTQ+ population and the disease we battled. Through that connection, these loved ones acknowledged the threat of AIDS in their immediate circle of friends. This movement combined with others to bring national awareness and action to the epidemic and ultimately transformed an HIV-positive diagnosis from a death sentence to a chronic illness.

Note "chronic illness." You can still get HIV. Put a condom on, George, or put it away! Or take PrEP? I'm not sure how all of this works these days, because my lazy ass has been married for over thirty years and all I know about HIV protection comes from pharmaceutical commercials.

My point is, now that we're in the 2020's, this day has become more about supporting queer folx and embracing who we are. Someone coming out of the closet today enters a world that is more accepting and safer than when I came out back in 1992.

Not that my coming out was traumatic. While it wasn't the easiest process I'd ever gone through, my friends and family were supportive, if occasionally confused.

It was as if I'd given them a handcrafted gift. Some were thrilled. Some expected it and were just waiting to see what color it would be. And the rest were wary. Did it go with the rest of their decor? Did I mean for it to be seasonal? How long until they could joke about it? Is there a receipt? No returns, Felicia!

Your Lesbian Friend is here to help you avoid the confusion with a quick refresher on what to do when a loved one comes out to you. Or, if you are the one thinking of coming out, some thoughts on how to build up your courage.

After all, I could use a helper on the "Lesbian Friend" front.

Let's start with what to do when someone comes out to you. Don't forget that the person coming out is super nervous, no matter how obvious the rainbow-bedecked, queer-friendly atmosphere. Your stack of *Out* magazines, library of queer history books, and occasional visit from your Lesbian Friend mean little in the face of perceived societal disapproval and internalized homophobia.

How can I explain internalized homophobia? Because you need to understand why someone you love unconditionally would be reluctant to reveal this part of themselves.

While we all thrill a bit to gain society's disapproval, internalized homophobia is just a fancy way to say you hate yourself for being queer. This hatred and fear of your queerness pushes you into isolation and depression. And our culture cements it into your psyche.

It comes from books banned in schools simply because they show queer people.

It comes from anti-trans laws being enacted.

It comes from referencing your wife's mother during a conversation at knit night and having the woman next to you insist that you meant to say "husband." (For the record, the rest of the group rolled their eyes at this poor creature as I explained what a lesbian was and that yes, I did have a marriage license.)

Be patient, even if you want to scream, "Oh honey, I know you're gay. Let's go to brunch and celebrate YOU figuring it out!" Allow your loved one the space and time to share in their own way.

Although a gentle, "What's up?" might be the key to unwrapping this eager package.

One very important thing.... Please remember not to say, "I love you anyway" or "Even if you're queer, we still love you." That "anyway" and "still" translate into "Your being is disgusting but I will love you despite this giant flaw. Look at how beneficent I am."

Yeah. I know that's not what you were saying. And now that landmine will be avoided.

You're welcome.

Stay simple. "I love you" is a good start. "How can I support you?" is even better.

And remember that brunch is always on the gay agenda. May I suggest a Monte Cristo with your Bellini?

But maybe you're looking for advice on how to come out. After all, this is an awkward moment. Usually, you're telling people you've known for a long time. They really should have noticed before now.

Take note from the above! Maybe they are dropping hints that it's okay to tell them. Did they give you a rainbow mug for your last birthday? Are you finding stray copies of *Page Boy* around the house? Is your best friend suggesting watching *Heartstoppers*?

But perhaps that adds pressure to the moment. From personal experience, I know that having someone say, "Oh! Is that all?" when you're coming out to them feels simultaneously like a relief and an annoyance. I mean, like, could you have maybe clued ME in on this?!

Though I must admit, the relief of having my queer identity acknowledged overtook the annoyance. My shoulders dropped as the tension of hiding dissipated. And then, joy raced through my body as I realized this friend would always love and support me.

When I look back at my coming out in the nineties, I wish I'd gotten the awkwardness out of the way in one evening with a big surprise party—but the surprise was for everyone else! If you go this route, you could even invite that person you're crushing on. And who knows what could happen next?

Of course, there's always the chance that things will not go well. The weight of the judgment of friends, family, and, if you are older, your children and grandchildren can feel overwhelming. If you feel alone as you communicate your sexuality or gender, reach out. This queer community you are entering is the bedrock of "found family."

We've been creating bonds with those who don't share our blood for millennia. Local LGBTQ+ community centers and cafés are great places to start. Online communities exist as well, and organizations like the It Gets Better Project and SAGE for LGBTQ+ elders can provide lifelines of connection.

A strong community of allies, both gay and straight, exists out in this world. They are the bulwark we rely upon to get us through troubling times. Even though things are so much better than they were, the world can still be a dangerous place. As queer people, we're fighting for our right to BE in the world. And today, more and more people are attempting to force us back into the closet and convince us that it's not even worth opening the door.

Too late, Charlie. We know better.

Join me in celebrating National Coming Out Day! Let's sweep those closets bare.

After all, the skeletons need room for their Halloween decorations.

And yes, Halloween is Gay Christmas.

·❤·❤·❤·❤·❤·

THE ITALIAN CREAM CAKE

After my Uncle Bud died, my Aunt Leola went on a cake-baking spree. She'd always been a baker, but now, each time her kids visited, they left with a cake. Birthdays meant a towering three-layer cake for anyone she knew, from her adored great-grandchildren to tellers in the bank where she'd worked for decades before retiring. The church bake sale ladies always asked for a plethora of her creations, and she enthusiastically provided as many as they requested. On a trip to Arkansas for another uncle's funeral, my wife and I returned to our modest room at the Super 8 with an orange layer cake, complete with tiny mandarins decorating the edge.

We did our best, but still left half a cake in the motel room. I might have tried harder if I'd realized it was the last "Leola" cake I'd eat.

Leola honed her cake mastery through fifty-eight years of marriage, which began after graduating high school. Like my grandmother, she took pride in providing delicious cakes, cookies, and candy for sales and prizes over the years. Both my aunt and uncle worked full-time jobs while raising three boys and a girl, but she always found the time to delight nieces, nephews, and grandchildren with sweet treats from the oven.

Like her mother before her, her specialty was the Italian Cream Cake. A staple in the South, this butter cake is stuffed with coconut and toasted pecans and topped with cream cheese frosting. My mother craved this treat each holiday. When I began making my own version, I packed one into a tin and carried it across the country to delight Mom for Christmas. When she declared it as good as my Aunt Leola's, my heart exploded with pride.

In the days after her husband passed away, my Aunt Leola confided that she woke up in the middle of the night and couldn't get back to sleep for missing him. Her mourning whirred through the beaters of her mixer and baked in the oven as the sun rose. Delicious cakes emerged, both from scratch and from mixes. Chocolate, Red Velvet, Italian Cream, yellow, white, strawberry, peach, orange. She froze the layers to preserve them until any barely cake-related event appeared. Her daughter despaired about the full freezer and worried about my aunt leaving the oven on.

But expressing her creativity through baking calmed my aunt's soul when she missed my uncle the most. None of us could bear to ask her to stop.

Plus, her cakes were sooooo tasty!

Aunt Leola finally stopped baking when her memories became a tattered quilt of time and space. For the last few years of her life, she lived in an assisted care lockdown facility. When she finally entered hospice care right after Thanksgiving 2019, I began to bake. One of my Italian Cream cakes had been promised for the annual holiday party at work. I softened butter and creamed it with sugar, adding egg after egg. As I alternated flour with buttermilk, the batter became smooth and thick. I slipped the pans into the oven and waited.

After the layers cooled, I secured them in plastic wrap and slid them into the freezer to hold until the day before the party. On that day, they'd defrost and then I'd ice the cake for the celebration, just like my Aunt Leola had taught me.

In the dark of a too-early morning, I received the call that she had died. I cried and made my plans to drive across Tennessee, returning to Arkansas for the funeral scheduled for Saturday. By Friday, I was on the road. The office Christmas party happened while I gathered with family at the viewing. As I chatted with my cousins, a text pinged into my phone with a picture of the joyous group, laughing and slightly tipsy on the comedy tour bus I'd booked for the occasion.

I thought of those cake layers in the freezer. The next week, I would make the frosting. The sugar would blend smoothly with cream cheese and butter. Toasted chopped pecans would be folded in, giving the cake a rustic look and flavor. Then, that cake would travel into the office for a special holiday dessert on a nothing-special kind of day.

From where I sat on a pew at the family church, I could look back and see the exact spot where my grandparents had placed themselves each Sunday. Aunt Leola and Uncle Bud had always sung in the church choir, and their ghosts whisked in and out of the music as the full choir sang. Two ministers spoke, the current pastor who'd known her only as an adult and another who'd been friends with her boys, telling stories of their rambunctious childhood and the kindness and support of my aunt and uncle.

Both of them mentioned Leola's Italian Cream cake, as did most of the mourners. Leola's baked creations, especially the crowning glory of that Italian Cream cake, remained legendary in her community. Even all these years after she'd made her last one, people still craved it, talked about it, rejoiced in the memory.

During the obligatory post-funeral lunch, my mother boasted about my Italian Cream cake, saying that it was as good as my aunt's. My proud smile beamed across the table as I treasured how each swirl of the spoon in my mixing bowl connected me to my Aunt Leola and our family's baking tradition.

·♥·♥·♥·♥·♥·

THE JOY OF A GRIM SMILE

For a long time, I loved watching Scandinavian noir. Our local PBS showed subtitled mysteries late at night, so we'd record them and watch these dark shows in the afternoon. During the height of my obsession, I watched so many of them on weekends that I learned tiny bits of Swedish.

I occasionally still say "Hey-hey" when greeting someone.

But the noir got a little too dark, too violent, too hopeless for me. As English-speaking entertainment companies began to catch up to that Scandinavian level of darkness, my passion for the style waned. Soon, my television was invaded by English versions of popular Swedish mysteries.

Part of me blames *The Girl with the Dragon Tattoo*. But also, I devoured those books and movies, both the Swedish and English versions.

I admit it. I'm part of the problem.

As my television relinquished its hold on these serious dramatic series, I realized I was looking for something fun. Was it because my life had gotten too serious? Because I'd started feeling unsettled and unhappy? After all, life is hard and injustice shows up everywhere and betrayal happens.

Why spend my leisure time watching other people go through the same struggles I'm confronting?

So I dove into cozy mysteries, murders happening in the bright sunshine with little blood and a quirky nun or bookseller or baker finding the evildoer. Friends gathered to investigate at well-tended homes where cats played with the balls of yarn used to connect the dots on their murder boards. Justice came served with cupcakes.

I avoided noir altogether until my wife began watching old detective movies on streaming services. These B movies were spawned by the popularity of hardboiled detectives and the auteurs of suspense.

And yet, they delighted me, these cut-rate Hitchcocks and generic Sam Spades. Their heroes threw quips with their punches and seduced with a sardonic grin. First, I fell in love with Torchy Blane, a fast-talking "girl reporter" who solved mysteries with her policeman boyfriend in the 1930's. Then *Lady in the Lake*, a Philip Marlowe movie directed by and starring Robert Montgomery, which tells the tale from Marlowe's point of view, ambled onto our television screen this past December.

Someone must have decided that it was a Christmas movie since part of the action takes place on December 25th.

Thanks, *Die Hard*.

Marlowe parried and volleyed quips as I ate my lunch, giggled, and got drawn into the twists and turns of the conspiracy.

While no one would mistake Torchy Blane for noir, hardboiled detectives such as Philip Marlowe and Sam Spade are stalwarts of American noir. And they have something that no Scandinavian detective ever considered.

Jokes.

Dashiell Hammett and Raymond Chandler (the authors who created those two classic detectives) understood the necessity of humor in their work. The darkness can only be borne with the leavening of laughter. They battle the danger with punchlines. These world-wise private eyes never get the girl because she's the one who's done the deed, and they turn her into the cops with a wry grin. They feel the tragedy and twist it into dark comedy.

And that comedy was what I needed. The modern noir driven by the despairing Scandinavians, pieces like *True Detective* and any Batman prequel based in Gotham City–all of these dramas had forgotten that intrinsic piece of their dark puzzle. Taking themselves too seriously was the key to their success, they thought.

Well, not for this girl. Give me Archie Goodwin deftly ejecting a suspect from Nero Wolfe's townhome with a kick and a zinger. Sing me to sleep with *City of Angels,* a Broadway musical that plays a mystery writer and his fictional detective off each other.

And let me relax by reading my latest discovery, the Pentecost and Parker mysteries by Stephen Spotswood. These novels recast Rex Stout's Nero Wolfe stories with women. Lillian Pentecost is the brilliant detective battling MS who rarely ventures into the field, while Willowjean "Will" Parker takes on the role of the streetwise aide de camp, doing the legwork and seducing anyone attractive. Embracing folks who are queer and disabled, this series astounds me with how much I delight in it.

So go on with your dark, depressing Scandinavian noir and all of its dark, depressing descendants.

Serve me my darkness with a grin.

·♥·♥·♥·♥·♥·

NOTHING IS CERTAIN BUT DISHES & LAUNDRY

" *but in this world nothing can be said to be certain, except*
••• *death and taxes." - Ben Franklin*

Even before I did my Googling and read the name of the person who coined this phrase, I knew it was a man. And Ben Franklin?

Of course. Witty dude who knew his audience.

Which was not women.

And though he loved many, many women, apparently none of them clued him in to the certainty of dishes and laundry.

(Yes, I know that not only women do dishes and laundry, but let's all acknowledge the persistence of gendered roles in housework.)

There are days I've gone through where it felt like I progressed directly from cooking one meal, to cleaning up after it, and then to repeating the process two more times. And all the while, my laundry machines washed and dried. Folding happened throughout the day as I grabbed a moment of tea and television.

At least I don't have to go to a stream and pound my panties on rocks or use a washtub to scrub-scrub-scrub away the stains on my shirts. Those days were how this charming classic of women's literature got created:

Wash on Monday

Iron on Tuesday

Mend on Wednesday

Churn on Thursday

Clean on Friday

Bake on Saturday

Rest on Sunday

Except for dishes. Dishes get done on Sunday. And all of the other days of the week. None of these days are without dish duty.

This "Rhyme for the Workhorse" (not its real name—did it ever have a title?) first came to my attention when I read *Little House in the Big Woods* by Laura Ingalls Wilder. This problematic but widely loved writer instilled a romantic view of many chores in my mind. My mother gave me the entire book series, and I fell in love with scenes like Laura and Mary knitting by the fire while snow whirled outside in the frigid South Dakota winter. Alonzo's mother weaving the fabric to make their clothes in *Farmer Boy*. Ma baking all of their bread from scratch.

Some of you might contest my assertion that dishes and laundry are inevitable. Perhaps you only eat on paper plates with plastic utensils and wipe your wasteful mouth with paper napkins. Besides the fact that Mother Earth thanks you every time you wash a reusable dish, tossing your plates in the trash still qualifies as doing the dishes. So, no! You still did the dishes.

Perhaps you believe that placing the dishes into the dishwasher doesn't count as doing dishes? But if doing the laundry includes putting clothes in the machine, Baby, I'm washing dishes every time I hit "go" on the dishwasher.

Plus, even when I fill up the dishwasher (which uses less water and is generally more efficient than handwashing), I end up doing some dishes by hand because I will want them before the next dishwasher operation. After all, even with four of us, we aren't running the dishwasher every day.

Though maybe we should?

My habit of wearing clothes, especially when the weather gets cold, means laundry happens once a week.

Laundry is one of my favorite chores because it can be done while I'm doing other things. Woohoo for the washing machine and dryer!! Two of the most magnificent inventions of all time! These magical machines alleviate the need for me to spend Monday scrubbing our clothes and hanging them out.

Actually, on a recent episode of *All Creatures Great & Small*, I saw

Mrs. Hall use an inside laundry drying rack that lifted up to the ceiling in the kitchen and thought, "How marvelous! What ingenuity!" When my wife and I first got together, we had a washer but no dryer and hung all of our clothes on a line outside. In the winter, they would come in stiff and hard until they melted a little and then would still need drying. How handy would that rack have been?

Anyway, I rarely purchase things that have to be hung up for drying, but when I do, I hang them up all around the house. They go on closet doors and towel hooks and places like that until they are dry, which is usually in only a day or so. Pants get tossed over doors, though that usually means cleaning a line of dust off the clean pants.

I probably should dust the tops of the doors more often. At least when I'm drying clothing across them.

My point is that a certain amount of privilege is necessary to think that only death and taxes are certain. Those who do their own dishes and laundry know that those things can never be avoided. In fact, we've all seen that not everyone has to pay taxes, but dishes and laundry always need to be done.

When I came out, there was one moment where I felt like I'd flung off the harness of traditional "women's work." But then, as I looked at this life that my sweetie and I were creating, I knew where I fit in.

I had to come to grips with the idea that even though I was a Lesbian (fuck you, patriarchy!) and an Author (tip-tap on the typewriter wrapped in a glamorous cape), I was also a Housewyfe.

And a happy Housewyfe, dang it.

So, dishes and laundry every darn day.

Get it right, Ben Franklin.

·♥·♥·♥·♥·♥·

HOW TO SURVIVE THE HOLIDAYS WITHOUT GETTING DRUNK

A few years ago, I stopped drinking by accident.

Not to say that I don't drink alcohol at all. On special occasions, we open an exquisite bottle of wine from our collection. If it's been a particularly alarming day, I might sip a finger of whiskey over ice to calm my body. A special meal at a nice restaurant means selecting a gorgeous glass of wine, a yummy local beer, or a cocktail magicked into being by the resident mixologist.

But, as a rule, I stick with water, seltzer (if I need bubbles), and tea.

At some point (during the pandemic? Before the pandemic? I don't remember), I discovered that drinking two nights in a row made LA a horrible bitch. I felt sad the whole next day, said mean things to people, and was basically a wretched person until the alcohol worked its way out of my system.

And that's not the way to spend the holidays! I want to feel good, happy, content. And I don't want anyone else worrying about me and my alcohol intake.

As in:

"Are you sure you don't want another drink?"

"Can I top you off?"

"Don't you want to try my special holiday cocktail?" (Which usually means, "Try this headache-inducing combination of alcohol and sugar.")

No, actually. I want to enjoy the holiday season!

And I figure there are other folks out there who want to do this too.

So here are my tricks for avoiding drinking too much during the holidays.

Having just one drink is an option. But this strategy is tricky, because once you've had just the one drink, you'll want another. And your liquor-addled brain will agree with you. Why not? It's the holidays, right? Plus, you're an adult! You get to do what you want.

Which was to avoid drinking too much.... Dang it.

So, how do I set a limit and stay within it?

1. Make an exception list. One cup of my wife's special eggnog brightens my Christmas Eve. That brandywine that's only available during the holidays? Perhaps a glass of that will be sipped as presents are wrapped. A hot toddy after dinner eases the symptoms of my first cold of the season.

Making decisions about how and where and why I'll indulge reduces the chance of overindulgence. When I do indulge, each delightful sip lingers on my tongue, blooming to reveal every nuance.

2. For years, I've been our designated driver. Because of this, I stay aware of the time. On average, the human body can metabolize about a drink an hour. This means that, if we want to leave a party early, sipping one drink over the course of an hour allows me to safely drive home at any time. Because I'm an introvert who is happy to leave a party even before getting there, the reward of escape works well for me.

Plus, I have an automatic out. My stroke-affected wife deals with partial paralysis, and her body decides when we leave. This moment of go-go-go comes in an instant. Everything can be fine and then suddenly, she'll droop. Her face will change in this unmistakable way and Boom! Time to go.

So she selects the timing. When she says go, we go. There's no dallying to say goodbye to the host. If they aren't there or easy to get to, too bad. We're off to the car while she can still make her partially paralyzed legs walk.

Ah, the relief! If I were an extrovert, this change would be frustrating. Instead, I'm happy to get the car and bundle her inside. "Oh, sorry! We've got to go!" I'll trill at our hosts. "My sweetie turned into a pumpkin."

But what if you are an extrovert? What if you love parties? What if nothing feels better to you than gathering with large numbers of friends at random houses?

Excuse me for a moment while I shudder.

3. Bubbles. Not champagne bubbles! Soda, seltzer, carbonated-non-alcoholic-cocktails sorts of bubbles.

Bubbles are festive. When you're drinking anything that sparkles, it's a party, a special moment, something wonderful is happening!

This trick worked for me when I started skipping the glass of wine with my evening meal. Just before eating, I pop the top on a seltzer. Poured into a wine glass, our regular dinner transforms into a magical reward for a day well-lived. Each sip of my lime seltzer (sometimes I go crazy and drink other flavors like mandarin orange or dragonfruit-berry) refreshes my palate for another bite of the delicious dinner I've created.

At a bar, an order of club soda with lime looks more sophisticated than it is, and no one needs to know there's no vodka in there.

The bottom line? It's your choice. And if you drink more than you wanted on a particularly jolly night, don't beat yourself up. Enjoy the evening.

After all, it's the holidays!

·♥·♥·♥·♥·♥·

ACKNOWLEDGEMENTS

Over the past three years, I chose to embrace a life of creativity and wonder, of joy and love and devotion to my creative expression and my family.

And you wondrous people who took the time to read these silly essays and now this book...You helped me do that.

Thank You.

While writing is something that I would do even if I failed miserably at it, your appreciation for my work transforms it into a glorious revelry.

Your eyes and hearts and minds and (hopefully) chuckles keep me writing.

I am so grateful for your encouragement.

And to all of my beta readers and reviewers.... Thank you so much for your honesty, graciousness, and generosity. You helped me make this book a reality.

Joanne Palmer, you are the best! Thank you for being the first reader of many of these pieces, one of my biggest cheerleaders, and appreciated advisor.

And thank you, Kate Krautkramer, for reading these pieces even when they are totally not your style!

Keegan Williams edited several of these pieces during my writing for OutFrontMagazine.com and their gentle nudges and reminders helped to keep me on the right track.

The fabulous Mindi Meltz edited these pieces with care and kindness and helped my voice to shine in every page of this book.

Carolina Gryffin made my cartoon character dreams come true when she manifested the Lesbian Housewyfe riding everywhere on her squeezy mop!

Occasionally a gift would show up in the mail from my fabulous friends, Nancy Paul and Janet Selbe. Thank you for your generosity.

A big thank you goes out to Beth Barany, founder of the WritersFunZone.com, novelist, and budding filmmaker, who generously shared her secrets of self-publishing with me and made this book possible.

To my parents, Barb, Monika, and Kathryn who supported us as I made this leap, thank you. Even though my mother passed before this collection was gathered, she read these essays and generously shared her reactions when possible.

And of course, my deepest love and gratitude to my sweet Stephanie. You are my first editor and best thing in my life.

·♥·♥·♥·♥·♥·

ABOUT THE AUTHOR

LA (as in tra-la-la) Bourgeois is the Lesbian Housewyfe, a lady who appreciates being called Ma'am and gets her hair painted with colorful stripes at the beauty parlor. She writes and coaches to support the family while caretaking for her stroke-affected wyfe and aging parents. She's one of Mack the dog's two mommies. Gardening, baking, knitting, and reading all continue to enthrall her (though she does watch a shit-ton of TV).

Despite a busy schedule, she manages to spend time with friends (who continue to endure her moodswings as she navigates the humid swamp-tits of menopause).

Her family escaped the south and ended up in Ithaca, New York, a city described in an online review as "a liberal cesspool."

Yes, please! What a refreshing change!

She identifies as a lesbian, anti-racist, sex-positive, trans-allied, white cis-woman who is politically liberal as hell but oh-so-tired of marching and calling my representatives. Pronouns are she/her/ma'am.

If you'd like to keep up with her newest adventures, subscribe to the *Diary of a Lesbian Housewyfe* newsletter at lesbianhousewyfe.su bstack.com.

·♥·♥·♥·♥·♥·

LAND ACKNOWLEDGEMENT

*T*his book was created in Western North Carolina on the homelands of the Tsalaguwetiyi (Cherokee, East), S'atsoyaha (Yuchi), and Miccosukee, and in Ithaca, New York, on Gayogohó□nǫ' (Cayuga) territory, part of the Haudeonsaunee Confederacy. I thank the indigenous stewards of this land and honor them through uplifting their sovereignty, protecting this beautiful landscape, and increasing their visibility as I am able.

www.ingramcontent.com/pod-product-compliance
Lightning Source LLC
Chambersburg PA
CBHW020158090426
42734CB00008B/869